Paris, the City of Light, is arguably the most beautiful city in the world. Are you not convinced? Then take a trip on the Seine as the river passes under the splendid Pont des Arts and Pont Alexandre-III, making its triumphal march past such wonders as **Notre-Dame**, the **Tuileries Garden**, the **Orsay Museum**, the **Eiffel Tower** and the **Palais de Chaillot**. The capital is surprisingly small, however, within the confines of its ring road: 11 miles from east to west, and less than 6 miles from north to south – in other words, a distance that can be covered on foot in two hours. It is sometimes said that Paris is a village, or at least a series of several villages, each with its own bakery, café, grocery store and square. This is the charm of a city that is both monumental and human. The Seine has two banks to explore, the **Left** and **Right Bank**, each with its own rhythm and lifestyle: the literary and increasingly fashionable **St-Germain**, the quintessentially Parisian **Montmartre** and **Pigalle**, the mixture of working class and yuppie **Canal St-Martin** and **Oberkampf**, the multicultural **Belleville**. On both sides, however, there is a wealth of cozy bistros, gourmet restaurants, unpretentious cafés, trendy boutiques, adventurous music venues, theaters and colorful street markets. All these, and more, are now within your reach, thanks to this **MapGuide**.

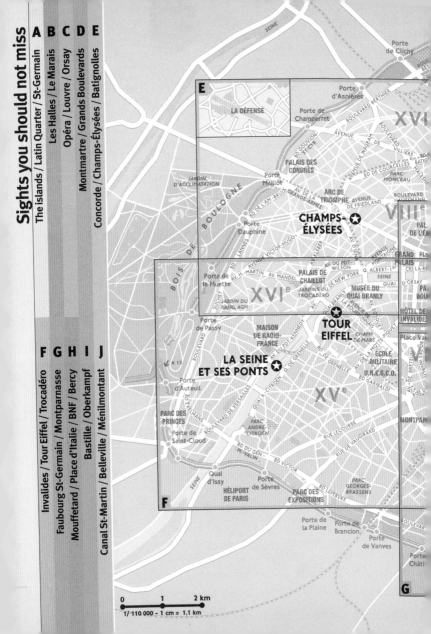

Sights you should not miss

A The Islands / Latin Quarter / St-Germain
B Les Halles / Le Marais
C Opéra / Louvre / Orsay
D Montmartre / Grands Boulevards
E Concorde / Champs-Élysées / Batignolles

F Invalides / Tour Eiffel / Trocadéro
G Faubourg St-Germain / Montparnasse
H Mouffetard / Place d'Italie / BNF / Bercy
I Bastille / Oberkampf
J Canal St-Martin / Belleville / Ménilmontant

0   1   2 km
1/ 110 000 - 1 cm = 1,1 km

The Île de la Cité is the historic and geographic heart of Paris, filled with remnants of the old royal city. On the Rive Gauche (Left Bank) is the Latin Quarter with its art-house cinemas, universities and publishing houses. Further south, the 'Boul' Mich' (Boulevard St-Michel) climbs toward the Luxembourg Gardens passing by the Sorbonne and the Rue Soufflot, which leads to a majestic Pantheon. To the west, the Place de l'Odéon has held onto its former elegance and the Rue St-André-des-Arts, to its medieval alleyways. Nearby is St-Germain-des-Prés with its postwar literary cafés and its very trendy boutiques.

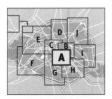

LE COMPTOIR

ISAMI

RESTAURANTS

Cosi (**A** B2)
→ 54, rue de Seine (6th)
Tel. 01 46 33 35 36
Daily noon–11pm
Delicious oven-baked bread and the freshest of produce to spread on it such as tapenade, salmon and pickled tomatoes. Good selection of wines by the glass. Sandwiches €5.50–8.50; prix fixe €9.50–12.

Le Petit St-Benoît (**A** B2)
→ 4, rue St-Benoît (6th)
Tel. 01 42 60 27 92; Tue-Sat noon–2.30pm, 7–10.30pm
A brasserie from 1901, run by the Gervais-Daffis family since 1960, where regulars keep their napkins in a tall cabinet with miniature drawers. Average home cooking (shepherd's pie, pot-au-feu) but the charm of a bygone age. Entrées €11.50–17.

Le Pré Verre (**A** D3)
→ 8, rue Thénard (5th)
Tel. 01 43 54 59 47; Tue-Sat noon–2pm, 7.30–10.30pm
The Delacourcelle brothers' superb neo-bistro, where the dishes seem to burst with flavor thanks to the subtle use of spices. Prix fixe €13.50 (lunch), €29.50.

Mon Vieil Ami (**A** E2)
→ 69, rue St-Louis-en-l'Île (4th); Tel. 01 40 46 01 35
Wed-Sun noon–3pm, 7–11pm
'My old friend' allies the traditional – oak beams from its former life as a tavern – with the contemporary: tables laid out with style in a black-and-cream spartan decor. The classic seasonal French cuisine gives pride of place to vegetables. Prix fixe €43; entrées €13 (lunch), €23.

L'Épi Dupin (**A** A2)
→ 11, rue Dupin (6th); Tel. 01 42 22 64 56; Mon 7–11pm; Tue-Fri noon–3pm, 3–5.30pm (tearoom), 7–11pm
In a small, modern space with stone walls and exposed whitewashed beams, François Pasteau and his team serve very good, imaginative French food. Prix fixe €24 (lunch), €34 (dinner).

Le Comptoir du Relais St-Germain (**A** C2)
→ 7, carrefour de l'Odéon (6th); Tel. 01 44 27 07 97
Mon-Fri noon–6pm, 8.30–10pm; Sat-Sun noon–11pm
Acclaimed bistro of Yves Camdeborde, the star of Parisian 'bistronomy', has a tiny dining room with retro decor and a sidewalk terrace. Sample

PONT-NEUF / PLACE DAUPHINE

CONCIERGERIE

STE-CHAPELLE

▲ Map C

A   B   C

PYRAMIDE

QUAI FRANÇOIS-MITTERRAND

LOUVRE
RIVOLI

RUE DE RIVO

Q. A.-FRANCE

PONT ROYAL

PONT DU
CARROUSEL

MUSÉE
DU LOUVRE

RUE DE L'AMIRAL-
DE-COLIGNY

ST-GERMAIN-
L'AUXERROIS

RUE DE LA
MONNAIE

MUSAY
D'ORSAY

R. DE LILLE

QUAI VOLTAIRE

S E I N E

QUAI DU LOUVRE

PONT-N

1   vie

RUE DU BAC

RUE DE BEAUNE

RUE DE LILLE

QUAI
MALAQUAIS

PONT
DES ARTS

PONT-
M

QUAI

RUE DE VERNEUIL

RUE DE L'UNIVERSITÉ

RUE DU
BAC

QUAI DE CONTI

RUE
MONTALEMBERT

RUE G.
GALLIMARD

ÉCOLE DES
BEAUX-ARTS

RUE DES
BEAUX-ARTS

INSTITUT
DE FRANCE

PONT-NEUF /
PLACE DAUPHINE

★ QUAI DE

Place Dauphine

SAINT-THOMAS-
D'AQUIN

RUE DES SAINTS-PÈRES

RUE DES
SAINTS-PÈRES

RUE DE SEINE

RUE JACOB

R. VISCONTI

HÔTEL
DES MONNAIES

RUE DE NEVERS

R. GUÉNÉGAUD

QUAI DES
GRANDS-AUGUSTINS

SAINT

BD SAINT-GERMAIN

RUE DU
AUX-CLERCS

UNIVERSITÉ
PARIS-V

RUE BONAPARTE

RUE JACOB

RUE DE
NESLE

QUAI DES
GRANDS-AUGUSTINS

QUAI
CHAPE

SAINT-VLADIMIR-
LE-GRAND

RUE ST-
BENOÎT

ÉGLISE
SAINT-GERMAIN-
DES-PRÉS

RUE MAZARINE

QUARTIER
LATIN

NOTRE-
ST-MIC
(R.E.R.)

2

RUE SAINT-
GUILLAUME

RUE DE LA
CHAISE

Place
Saint-Germain-
des-Prés

M

Place de
Furstemberg

RUE DE
BUCI

RUE DE
L'ANCIENNE
COMÉDIE

RUE ST-ANDRÉ-DES-ARTS

RUE DE
L'ÉPERON

RUE
HAUTEFE

RUE DE GRENELLE

ST-GERMAIN-
DES-PRÉS

MABILLON

M

BD DE SEINE

BD SAINT-GERMAIN

RUE DANTON

SQUARE
CHAISE-
RÉCAMIER

RUE DU DRAGON

RUE DU FOUR

RUE DU FOUR

RUE
MABILLON

RUE
CLÉMENT

RUE
SERPENTE

R. DE SÈVRES

RUE DU
VIEUX-COLOMBIER

RUE PRINCESSE

RUE DES
CANETTES

RUE DE SEINE

RUE DES
QUATRE-
VENTS

ODÉON

M

Carrefour
de l'Odéon

R. DE L'ÉCOLE-DE-MÉDECINE

UNIVERSITÉ PARIS-V
R.-DESCARTES

SÈVRES-
BABYLONE

M

ST-SULPICE

M

RUE DU
CHERCHE-MIDI

RUE
BONAPARTE

Place
Saint-Sulpice

R. GUISARDE

★

RUE GARANCIÈRE

R. ST-SULPICE

R. DE CONDÉ

R. DE L'ODÉON

R. DE TOURNON

SARRAZIN

UNIVERSITÉ
PARIS-VI

RUE RACINE

MONSIEUR-LE

MICHEL

PL.

3

BOULEVA

RUE DE RENNES

RUE DE MÉZIÈRES

ÉGLISE SAINT-
SULPICE

vie

RUE
COËTLOGON

RUE
CASSETTE

RUE
MADAME

SAINT-
JOSEPH

Place de
l'Odéon

THÉÂTRE DE
L'ODÉON

RUE DE VAUGIRA

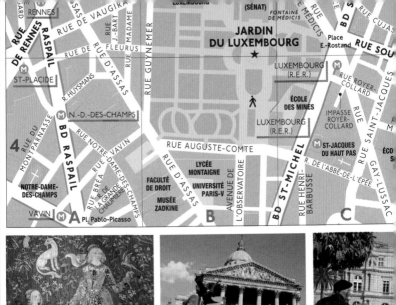

THERMES AND HÔTEL DE CLUNY

PANTHÉON

JARDIN DU LUXEMBOURG

★ **Pont-Neuf /
Place Dauphine** (A C1)
The oldest and most
famous of Paris's bridges
was completed in 1604 to
allow King Henry IV to cross
from one bank to the other.
At the far end of the Île de
la Cité is Place Dauphine,
the second of the capital's
royal squares, built in 1607
in honor of the Dauphin.

★ **Conciergerie** (A D2)
➜ 2, bd du Palais (1st)
Tel. 01 53 40 60 97
Daily 9.30am–5.30pm
The north wing of the huge
Palais de Justice where, as
far back as the 14th century,
the concierge was the officer
in charge of the building

and its prison. You can see
the guardroom (14th c.)
and the ancient cells where
Queen Marie-Antoinette
spent her last days.

★ **Ste-Chapelle** (A D2)
➜ 6, bd du Palais (1st)
Daily 9.30am (9am in
winter)–5pm
This Gothic architectural
gem was built at the
request of St Louis (1245–8)
to house Christ's Crown of
Thorns. The use of
abutments, instead of flying
buttresses, and metal
frames and iron clamps
enabled the construction
of the extraordinary 50-ft-
high stained-glass windows
that stand out against the

extremely narrow building.
They depict some 1,134
scenes from the Old and
New Testaments along with
the story of Louis IX
receiving the holy relics.

★ **Cathédrale
Notre-Dame** (A E2)
➜ 6, pl. du Parvis-Notre-Dame
(4th); Tel. 01 42 34 56 10
Daily 7.45am–7pm
An impressive cathedral
begun in 1163. Here the
use of flying buttresses
permitted windows to be
introduced on a scale that
was previously unheard of.
The beautiful rose window
to the south, the delicacy
of the buttresses and the
fragility of the spire make

this a true masterpiece
Gothic architecture.

★ **Île St-Louis** (A E2)
Two islets used as pas
land were joined togeth
to form this tiny island
when Christophe Marie
engineer to Louis XIII,
began building a villag
here in 1614. More intir
than its neighbor, the Î
la Cité, it is full of supe
old town houses, narro
streets and flights of st
leading down to the Se

★ **Thermes and Hôte
Cluny / Musée Nati
du Moyen Âge** (A C3
➜ 6, pl. Paul-Painlevé (5
Tel. 01 53 73 78 00
Wed–Mon 9.15am–5.45p

CAFÉ CHARBON, RUE OBERKAMPF

PALAIS-ROYAL

CENTRE POMPIDOU

closer to restaurants than cafés. These 'neo-bistros' serve high-quality, revamped traditional cuisine: the French version of the British gastropub.

Brasserie
It serves seafood, steak and fries, choucroute (sauerkraut with pork, potato, sausage, ham) and other typical dishes, with wine or beer. It provides an all-day service.

Restaurant
French or foreign cuisine and often a well-stocked cellar. Reservations are necessary.

Cookery classes
L'Atelier des Chefs
→ atelierdeschefs.fr
Learn to cook with a variety of classes, from lunch sessions to parent-child classes or sushi initiations. Six venues in Paris.

With toddlers
Le Poussette café (D C5)
→ 6, rue Pierre-Sémard (9th)

Tel. 01 78 10 49 00
Tue-Sat 10.30am–6.30pm
Children's menu, story-time, magicians and workshops for parents.
Les 400 coups (J C4)
→ 12bis, rue de la Villette (19th); Tel. 01 40 40 77 78; Mon-Tue, Thu-Fri noon–3pm; Wed, Sat-Sun 10.30am–6pm
Children's menus and afternoon tea, but also workshops and games.

GOING OUT

Latin Quarter and **St-Germain** (A C2): jazzy, student quarter.
Le Marais (B D3): the gay district.
Bercy, Tolbiac (H E3): nightlife on the waterfront.
Oberkampf (I B1), **Canal Saint-Martin** (J A5), **Ménilmontant** (J C6): attract a new generation of party animals.
Bastille (I B3): for a classic Parisian nightlife.

SHOWS

Reservations
Fnac
→ Tel. 08 92 68 36 22; Mon-Sat 9am–7pm (1pm Sat) fnacspectacles.com
Virgin Méga Store
→ Tel. 08 25 02 30 24 Mon-Sat 9am–7pm; virginmega.fr

Discounts
Kiosque Jeunes (13- to 28-year-olds)
→ 101, quai Branly (F D2) Tel. 01 43 06 15 38 Mon-Wed, Fri 10am–1pm, 2–6pm; Thu 1–6pm
→ 14, rue F.-Miron (B C4) Tel. 01 42 71 38 76 Mon-Fri 10am–7pm; jeunes.paris.fr

Theater kiosks
→ Pl. de la Madeleine (C C2)
→ Pl. des Ternes (E D2)
→ Esplanade Montparnasse (G B3)
All open Tue-Sun 12.30–8pm (4pm Sun)
Fifty percent reduction for

same-day performances.
Private theaters
Most will sell €10 tickets to the under 26s, one hour before performances.

Programs
Officiel des Spectacles and Pariscope
→ Out every Wed, on sale at newsagents
Listings of cultural events.

SHOPPING

Department stores
BHV (B C3)
→ 52, rue de Rivoli (4th)
A mecca for DIY.
Galeries Lafayette (D A6)
→ 40 bd Haussmann (9th)
and Printemps (D A6)
→ 64, bd Haussmann (9th)
The biggest and increasingly luxurious.
Le Bon Marché (G B1)
→ 24, rue de Sèvres (7th)
The most elegant.

Flea markets
Puces de St-Ouen (off D A1)
→ Métro Porte-de-

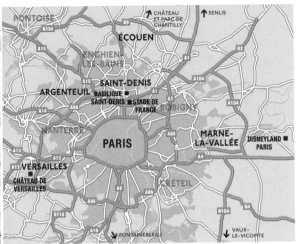

EXCURSIONS

MUSEUMS

Children
Some museums offer games, tours, workshops.

Concessions
Usually for students, 18–25-year-olds, the over 60s and the unemployed.

Musée du Louvre (C E3)
→ *Reduced rates Wed and Fri after 6pm*

Free admission
National museums
→ *First Sun of the month for all; daily for the under 26s visiting permanent collections*

City museums
→ *Daily for visits to permanent exhibitions*

Paris Museum Pass
→ *Pass available from participating museums, FNAC, tourist offices, etc. Two-, four- or six-day card (€39, €54, €69)*
Free admission to more than 60 museums and sites in and around Paris.

Clignancourt
Sat–Mon 7am–7.30pm
The oldest and biggest of the city's flea markets.

Puces de Montreuil
(off **I** F2)
→ *Métro Porte-de-Montreuil Sat–Mon 7am–7.30pm*
With St-Ouen, the most popular market, selling cheap clothes, DIY equipment, knick-knacks.

Puces de Vanves (off **G** A5)
→ *Av. G.-Lafenestre Métro Porte-de-Vanves Sat–Sun 7am–7.30pm*
Interesting bric-à-brac and reasonably priced antiques.

Food markets
Place Maubert (5th) (A D3)
→ *Tue, Thu, Sat 7am–2.30pm*
Bd R.-Lenoir (11th) (I B2)
→ *Thu, Sun 7am–3pm*
Rue d'Aligre (12th) (I C3)
→ *Tue–Sun 7am–1.30pm*
Bd de Belleville (20th)
(**J** B5)
→ *Tue, Fri 7am–2.30pm*
Sales
Jan and end June–beg July.

Guided tours
Centre des Monuments Nationaux (H C1)
→ *Hotel Sully, 62 rue St-Antoine (4th) Tel. 01 44 54 19 30*
Visits to some sites usually closed to the public.

Amicale Inter Guides (E F1)
→ *108, rue Legendre (17th) Tel. 01 42 28 98 58 amicaleinterguides@yahoo.fr*
Tailor-made tours with guide-interpreters.

GREEN SPACES

Paris has over 460 parks and gardens.

Bois de Boulogne (F A1-3)
→ *Métro Porte-Maillot*
Bicycle rental at the Jardin d'Acclimatation entrance.

Bois de Vincennes (off **I** F4)
→ *Métro Château-de-Vincennes*
Cycle tracks, bridlepaths and pedestrian pathways.

EXCURSIONS

Stade de France
→ *Line 13, St-Denis–Porte de Paris stop*
Opened in 1998 for the football World Cup.

Basilique St-Denis
→ *Line 13, Basilique St-Denis stop*
Gothic work of art and burial ground for all the kings of France.

Écouen
→ *Gare du Nord, Écouen-Ézanville stop*
National museum of the Renaissance; set in a Renaissance castle.

Chantilly chateau and park
→ *Gare du Nord, Chantilly stop*
Idyllic 19th-century palace: paintings by Raphael and Corot, French-style garden.

Senlis
→ *RER D to Orry-la-Ville*
A beautiful little town with narrow medieval streets.

Disneyland Paris
→ *RER A to Marne-la-Vallée*
The magic atmosphere of the world of Mickey Mouse and the Lion King.

Vaux-le-Vicomte
→ *RER D to Melun then Chateaubus shuttle*
Fouquet's castle (1661), which made Louis IV green with envy.

Fontainebleau
→ *Gare de Lyon, Fontainebleau-Avon stop*
Sumptuous Renaissance castle with splendid frescoes, right by the forest.

Château de Versailles
→ *RER C to Versailles-Rive-Gauche*
The magnificent palace of the Sun King (17th c.).

PONT DES ARTS

PARC DE LA VILLETTE

EIFFEL TOWER

ST-GERMAIN-DES-PRÉS

MONTMARTRE

Top ten

Paris sights you should not miss

✪ The islands (A C1-F3)
In the beginning were the islands: the Île de la Cité and Île St-Louis. The former became the seat of political, judicial and religious power back in the 3rd century and has the imposing Cathedral of Notre-Dame as its dominant feature. In its shadow, the Île St-Louis boasts romantic alleyways and quays that are favorite spots for picnickers.

✪ The Seine and its bridges
The Seine runs for over 8 miles through Paris, spanned by bridges that evoke the city's cultural history just as much as its monuments, with memories of Juliette Binoche on the Pont-Neuf in *The Lovers on the Bridge*, of the 1900 Universal Exhibition on the Pont Alexandre-III, of Apollinaire's poem 'Le Pont Mirabeau'... Couples declare their undying love on the Pont des Arts, with padlocks attached to the railing, while the reflection of the Eiffel Tower can be admired from the Pont d'Iéna.

✪ Latin Quarter (A)
This district is 'Latin' because classes were taught in this language in the university back in the 13th century. The Rive Gauche is still the city's academic hub, thanks to the Sorbonne, the Collège de France and the Lycée Henri-IV. In May 1968 the Boulevard St-Michel resounded with the slogans of revolt, and today students still argue for a better world in the bars on Montagne Ste-Geneviève.

✪ The Marais (B)
This former swamp was reclaimed in the 13th century and 400 years later it became a haunt of high society, with private hotels springing up around the Place des Vosges. These days it boasts an impressive array of bars, as well as hosting substantial Jewish (Rue des Rosiers) and gay communities.

✪ Montmartre (D)
In the late 19th century, the slopes of this 425-ft-high hill, then dotted with windmills and vineyards, attracted such artistic figures as Renoir, Pissarro, and Toulouse-Lautrec. This was the age of *guinguettes*, dance halls and cabarets, and though it is sometimes viewed through rose-tinted glasses it remains, with its steep, cobble-stoned alleyways a few yards away from the crowded Sacré-Cœur and Place du Tertre, one of the last of the Parisian 'villages'.

✪ Eiffel Tower (F D1)
Engineer Gustave Eiffel's emblematic masterpiece, built for the 1889 Universal Exhibition. 1,050 ft high, made of 18,000 pieces of iron and 2.5 million rivets, its impact varies according to the vantage point – majestic from the Trocadéro, breathtakingly beautiful from its foot – while the interior offers a stunning view of Paris. At night it is illuminated by no less than 20,000 light bulbs (first five minutes of every hour until 2am, 1am in winter). Go up by foot (south pillar, 1,665 steps) or by elevator to floors one (museum and short documentary film), two and three (Eiffel's office).

✪ The great museums: Louvre (C E3), **Orsay (C** C4), **Centre Pompidou (B** C3)
Paris would be worth a visit for these three museums alone. The Louvre presents an artistic survey running from antiquity to 1848, including such masterpieces as the *Mona Lisa*. Orsay takes over for the period from 1848 to 1914, dominated by stunning Impressionist and Post-Impressionist collections. And the Centre Pompidou explores the art of the 20th century, starting with Rogers' and Piano's building itself.

✪ Champs-Élysées (E D3-F4)
The most beautiful, the most prestigious and the most expensive avenue in Paris was conceived to create a view worthy of the Sun King. It was then developed over the centuries to form part of the awe-inspiring thoroughfare linking the Louvre, the Place de la Concorde, the Arc de Triomphe and the Grande Arche de la Défense. Crowds flock to see the lights along the Champs-Élysées at Christmas.

✪ Parc de la Villette and the canals (J)
The Canal St-Martin and Canal de l'Ourcq, extending from the Bastille to La Villette, were first built by Napoleon to provide Paris with drinking water. They were overhauled in the 1990s and re-emerged with a series of delightful walkways, locks, cafés and modern stores. At the far end, the Parc de la Villette provides numerous attractions: thematic gardens, lawns dotted with red architectural follies, arts and science complexes, concerts and movies (open-air in summer).

✪ St-Germain-des-Prés (A)
This neighborhood owes its name to its 6th-century abbey, but it owes its legend to the world of art and literature: after World War Two, Jean-Paul Sartre and Simone de Beauvoir expounded on existentialism in the Café de Flore, while Boris Vian tried out new songs in the jazz clubs. The spirit of these days can be recaptured in its back-streets and bookshops, although these now have to co-exist with major fashion labels.

CITY PROFILE

- 2.2 million inh. in the city center (11.5 million in metropolitan area)
- Third most populated city in Europe
- 20 arrondissements
- 40 square miles
- The most visited city in the world, with 28 million visitors in 2010
- 219 theaters, 173 museums
- 10,500 cafés and restaurants, 1,465 hotels
- 8 miles of River Seine
- 37 bridges
- Highest point: 426 ft (Montmartre)
- The banks of the River Seine are on UNESCO's World Heritage Sites list

THE HOLY TRINITY AND EIFFEL TOWER AT SUNSET

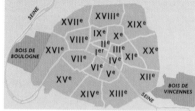
THE 20 ARRONDISSEMENTS (DISTRICTS) OF PARIS

LUTETIA TO PARIS

52 BC Roman legions conquer the Parisii **508** Clovis makes Paris the capital city of the Franks **1572** St Bartholomew's Day Massacre **1789** Fall of the Bastille **1841** Thiers builds a defensive wall around Paris, defining the city limits **1860** Haussmann rebuilds much of the city, which moves from 12 to 20 arrondissements **May 1871** The Commune: Paris in revolt **1900** Olympic Games and Universal Exhibition **Aug 1944** Liberation of Paris **May 1968** Barricades in the Latin Quarter

WWW.

→ *parisinfo.com*
Website of the tourist office.
→ *paris.fr*
The city's official website with detailed information on festivals, events, etc.
→ *parisnightlife.fr*
→ *sortiraparis.com*
Going out in the capital.
Internet cafés
Milk Internet Hall
→ *17, rue Soufflot* (**A** C3)
→ *31, bd Sébastopol* (**B** C2)
→ *28, rue du Quatre-Septembre* (**C** E2)
→ *5, rue d'Odessa* (**G** B3)
Cybercafés open 24/7.

TOURIST INFO

Office du Tourisme et des Congrès (**C** D3)
→ *25, rue des Pyramides (1st); No telephone*
Daily 10am (11am Sun)–7pm
Information, reservations, excursions. Other branches Gare du Nord, Gare de l'Est, Gare de Lyon, Métro Anvers and Porte de Versailles. April-Oct, kiosks in the Champs-Élysées and in front of Notre-Dame. July-Aug, Place de l'Hôtel-de-Ville and Place de la Bastille. Tourist information Place du Tertre.

TELEPHONE

Useful numbers
Police
→ *Tel. 17*
Pompiers (fire brigade)
→ *Tel. 18*
Samu (ambulance)
→ *Tel. 15, 112 (cell phone)*
Directory inquiries
→ *Tel. 118 712 / 118 218*
Lost property
→ *Tel. 08 21 00 25 25*

DIARY OF EVENTS

March-May
Banlieues Bleues
→ *Mid-March-mid-April;*

banlieuesbleues.org
Jazz festival in Seine-St-Denis (northern suburbs).
Paris Marathon
→ *Early April; parismarathon.com*
From the Champs-Élysées to Avenue Foch via Bastille and Bois de Vincennes.
Museum Night
→ *Mid-May; nuitdesmusees.culture.fr*
Tours by night; free entry.
June
Paris Jazz Festival
→ *Early June-end July; parisjazzfestival.fr*
In the Parc de Vincennes.
Fête de la Musique
→ *June 21; fetedelamusique.culture.fr*
Free concerts throughout the city. Listings in the daily newspapers.
Gay Pride
→ *End June; gaypride.fr*
Festival Solidays
→ *Three days, last weekend in June; solidays.org*
Associations and artists

against AIDS gather at the Longchamp racecourse.
July-August
National Day
→ *July 14*
Firemen's ball. Military parade down the Champs-Élysées and fireworks.
Paris Quartiers d'Été
→ *Mid-July-beg Aug; quartierdete.com*
Theater, dance, concerts in all the city's districts.
La Villette Film Festival
→ *Mid-July-mid-Aug*
In the Parc de la Villette (**J** D2), the largest open-air movie theater in Paris.
Paris-Plage
→ *Four to five weeks, mid-July-end Aug*
Sand, umbrellas and deckchairs are imported to the banks of the Seine to create beaches.
September
La Villette Jazz Festival
→ *First two weeks; jazzalavillette.com*
Fête des Jardins

THE INVALIDES AS SEEN FROM THE TOP OF THE MONTPARNASSE TOWER

→ *One weekend end Sep*
Garden show with guided tours, walks, workshops.
Heritage Open Days
→ *Third weekend; journeesdupatrimoine. culture.fr*
Free entry to monuments usually closed to the public.
Festival d'Automne
→ *Mid-Sep-end Dec; festival-automne.com*
Dance, theater, music, etc. celebrate fall.

October
Fête des Vendanges de Montmartre
→ *First or second weekend*
Parades of brotherhoods in Montmartre, celebrating the new vintage.
Nuit Blanche
→ *Early Oct (7pm-7am)*
A night of free cultural events in the most unusual places (swimming pools, churches, libraries).
Foire Internationale d'Art Contemporain (FIAC)
→ *End Oct; fiac.com*

The most important contemporary art event in France.

THE PRICE OF THINGS

A double room in a two-star hotel: €70–100; a main course in a brasserie: €10–15; a prix fixe in a neo-bistro €30–35; entry to a museum: €7; a beer: €2.50–4.50; an espresso: €1.50–3; entry to a club: €10–25.

OPENING TIMES

Shops
→ *Mon-Sat 9.30am-7pm; sometimes closed on Mon (not department stores). Late-night shopping on Thu in large department stores*
Museums
→ *Usually 10am-6pm. City museums usually close on Mon; national museums on Tue. Some operate a late-*

night opening
Parks and gardens
→ *Usually daily 8am (9am Sat-Sun)–sunset*
Banks
→ *Mon-Sat 9am-4 or 5pm*
Open 24/7
Pharmacie Derhy (**E** D3)
→ *84, av. des Champs-Élysées (8th)*
Tel. 01 45 62 02 41
Chemist.
Poste du Louvre (**B** A2)
→ *52, rue du Louvre (1st)*
Tel. 36 31; Daily 6am-7pm
Central post office.

EATING OUT

Establishments
Boulangerie (bakery)
It sells croissants, pains au chocolat, baguettes and sandwiches.
Bistro and neo-bistro
Ideal for a quick snack (croque-monsieur, salad, omelet, sandwich) served with a wine pitcher. Many bistros, however, are

ARCHITECTURE

Gothic Paris
(12th–beg 16th c.)
High gothic chapels, ogival vaulted ceilings and gothic arches; Notre-Dame (**A** E2).
Classical Paris
(17th–18th c.)
Town houses and other impressive buildings: symmetry and sobriety of decor; Invalides (**F** F2).
Haussmann's Paris
(second half of 19th c.)
Préfet from 1853 to 1870, Baron Haussmann modified the Parisian urban landscape, which had remained unchanged since the Middle Ages. He introduced the use of freestone, improvements to the sewage system, created parks and gardens, and the Grands Boulevards, large thoroughfares of subdued monumentality; Boulevard St-Germain (**A** A2-E3), Luxembourg Gardens (**A** B3).
Art Nouveau Paris
(1893–1912)
Blend of innovating materials, curved shapes and asymmetry, dear to Hector Guimard; Abbesses subway station (**D** B4).
Art Deco Paris
(1912–39)
Pure, geometric shapes and massive volumes; Palais de Chaillot (**F** D1).
Contemporary Paris
(1970–present)
Large works following post-modernist lines; Bibliothèque Nationale de France, or BNF (**H** D3); Musée du Quai-Branly (**F** D1).

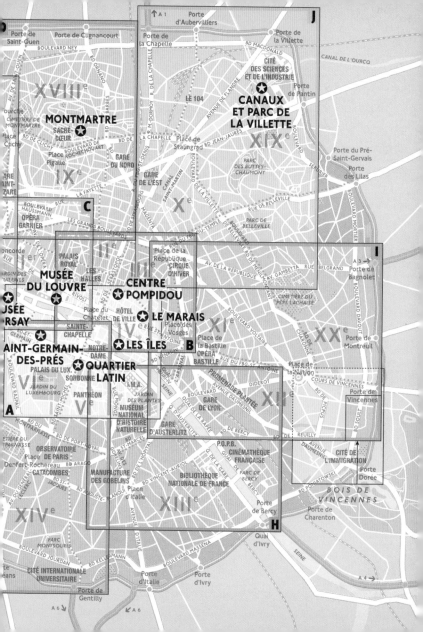

DEUX MAGOTS

WAGG

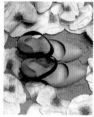

VANESSA BRUNO

the brasserie menu (daytime and weekend) or a more elaborate dinner (weekdays, reserve). At no. 3 l'Avant-Comptoir is a crêperie and 'hors d'oeuvres bar'. Entrées €16–25; prix-fixe dinner €50.

Isami (A E3)
→ 4, quai d'Orléans (4th)
Tel. 01 40 46 06 97; Tue-Sat noon–2pm, 7–10pm
One of the best sushi-ya (sushi bars) in Paris, with a dining room facing the Pont de la Tournelle.
Entrées €25–38.

TEAROOM, CAFÉS, ICE-CREAM PARLOR

La Pâtisserie Viennoise (A C3)
→ 8, rue de l'École-de-Médecine (6th)
Mon-Fri 8.30am–7.30pm
A tiny patisserie-tearoom, where a mixed crowd of students and tourists come on a daily basis for the delicious strudels and Viennese hot chocolates. Homemade pasta and salads at lunchtime.

Les Deux Magots (A B2)
→ 6, pl. St-Germain-des-Prés (6th); Daily 7.30am–1am
With the Flore, 50 yards down (172, bd St-Germain), Paris's most famous literary café. Both were

once the stronghold of Left Bank figures and existentialists – Picasso Hemingway, Sartre, De Beauvoir... Sit on the shady terrace giving onto the Place St-Germain-des-Prés. Pricey, but a truly Parisian experience.

Café de la Mairie (A B3)
→ 8, pl. St-Sulpice (6th)
Mon-Sat 7am (8am Sat)– 2am; Sun 9am–9pm
Off the tourist track that is the Boulevard St-Germain, it has a pleasant terrace opposite the church of St-Sulpice. The ashes of writer Nina Berberova were scattered under the plane tree at the front.

Berthillon (A F3)
→ 29-31, rue St-Louis-en-l'Île (4th); Tel. 01 43 54 31 61
Wed-Sun 10am–8pm; closed mid-July-Sep
The most celebrated ice-cream parlor in Paris is also a tearoom. Seven other outlets on the island in summer, when the main shop is closed.

CONCERTS, CLUBS

Caveau de la Huchette (A D2)
→ 5, rue de la Huchette (5th)
Tel. 01 43 26 65 05
Daily 9.30am–2.30am (sunrise Thu-Sat)
For the last 65 years this

medieval cellar has shown the wonders of jazz; live music from 10.15pm, swing, blues, soul at the end of the night.

Wagg (A B2)
→ 62, rue Mazarine (6th)
Tel. 01 55 42 22 01; Fri-Sat 11.30pm–6.45am; Sun 3pm–midnight (salsa classes 3–5pm)
It's as if the notorious 1960s club, the Whisky à Gogo, had come back to life. It still has the same lovely vaulted cellar, but now mainly plays funky music or disco. Salsa on Sundays.

SHOPPING

Bouquinistes (A C2-E3)
→ Depending on weather
These second-hand book stalls have stood on the banks of the Seine since the 19th century, filled with treasures for bargain-hunters: forgotten novels, old magazines, antique posters and cards.

Pierre Hermé (A B2)
→ 72, rue Bonaparte (6th)
Tel. 01 43 54 47 77; Daily 10am–7pm (7.30pm Thu-Fri; 8pm Sat)
Queues sometimes form outside this patisserie, whose black façade resembles a luxury jeweler. The biscuits,

macarons and cakes of the 'Picasso of pastry', as Hermé is known, are out of this world.

Fashion in St-Germain-des-Prés (A B2)
Designers and fashion boutiques wherever you look, in the epicenter of Parisian chic.

Vanessa Bruno (A B3)
→ 25, rue St-Sulpice (6th)
Tel. 01 43 54 41 04
Mon-Sat 10.30am–7.30pm
Inspired by her beloved Paris, Vanessa Bruno creates clothes for women that are simple, easy to wear, yet chic and sexy.

Dona Giacometti (A B3)
→ 6, rue St-Sulpice (6th)
Tel. 01 44 07 39 13
Tue-Sat 11am–7pm
Contemporary jewelry in glass, stone, gold and silver created by Dona herself in her boutique.

APC (A A3)
→ 38, rue Madame (6th)
Tel. 01 42 22 12 77
Mon-Sat 11am–7.30pm; Sun 12.30–6.30pm
Classic jeans and smartly cut jackets.

Les Prairies de Paris (A A2)
→ 6, rue du Pré-aux-Clercs (7th); Tel. 01 40 20 44 12
Mon-Fri 11am–2pm, 3–7pm; Sat 11am–7pm
The feminine creations of Laetitia Ivanez: tops, skirts, shoes, etc.

CATHÉDRALE NOTRE-DAME

ÎLE ST-LOUIS

CENTRE GEORGES-POMPIDOU

RAMBUTEAU

RUE DES INNOCENTS

RUE QUINCAMPOIX

RUE SAINT-DENIS

RUE SAINT-MARTIN

RUE ST-MERRI

SAINT-MERRI

RUE DE LA VERRERIE

BEAUBOURG

RUE DU RENARD

R. RAMBUTEAU

RUE DES ARCHIVES

RUE DES 4-FILS

RUE CHARLOT

CATHÉDRALE SAINTE-CROIX

RUE DE LA PERLE

RUE DU TEMPLE

RUE DES BLANCS-MANTEAUX

RUE SAINTE-CROIX-DE-LA-BRETONNERIE

RUE DES BLANCS-

RUE VIEILLE-DU-TEMPLE

RUE BARBETTE

RUE ELZEVIR

ARCHIVES NATIONALES

1

RUE FRANCS-BOURGEOIS

BOULEVARD DE SÉBASTOPOL

RUE DE RIVOLI

AVENUE VICTORIA

HÔTEL-DE-VILLE

CHÂTELET

HÔTEL DE VILLE

RUE DE LA VERRERIE

RUE MOUSSY

RUE DU BOURG-TIBOURG

RUE DES ROSIERS

RUE DES ECOUFFES

RUE PAVÉE

RUE E-DUVAL

LE MARAIS

QUAI DE GESVRES

QUAI DE MÉGISSERIE

CIERGERIE

RUE DE LOBAU

RUE F.-MIRON

SAINT-GERVAIS-SAINT-PROTAIS

RUE DU ROI-DE-SICILE

RUE DE RIVOLI

RUE ST-ANTOINE

BD DU PALAIS

QUAI DE LA CORSE

CITÉ

Place L.-Lépine

RUE DE LA CITÉ

HÔTEL-DIEU

QUAI DE L'HÔTEL-DE-VILLE

RUE DE L'HÔTEL-DE-VILLE

R. G.-LASNIER

R. DE JOUY

ST-PAUL

SAINT-PAUL-SAINT-LOUIS

RUE CHARLEMAGNE

PRÉFECTURE DE POLICE

R. D'ARCOLE

ÎLE DE LA CITÉ

IVe

PONT-MARIE

HÔTEL DE SENS

RUE DU FAUCONNIER

RUE DE L'AVE MARIA

RUE ST-PAUL

2

QUAI ST-MICHEL

RUE DE LA HUCHETTE

Place du Parvis-Notre-Dame

CATHÉDRALE NOTRE-DAME

RUE AUX FLEURS

PONT ST-LOUIS

PONT LOUIS-PHILIPPE

ÎLE SAINT-LOUIS

PONT MARIE

Q. DES CÉLESTINS

SAINT-SÉVERIN

RUE ST-JULIEN-LE-PAUVRE

SQUARE JEAN-XXIII

RUE SAINT-

QUAI D'ANJOU

SAINT-JULIEN-LE-PAUVRE

RUE DANTE

DE MONTEBELLO

PORT DE MONTEBELLO

PONT DE L'ARCHEVÊCHE

QUAI D'ORLÉANS

RUE DES DEUX-PONTS

LOUIS-EN-L'ÎLE

ST-LOUIS-EN-L'ÎLE

BD HENRI-IV

PONT DE SULLY

THERMES ET HÔTEL DE CLUNY

RUE THÉNARD

RUE DU SOMMERARD

RUE DE BIÈVRE

QUAI DE LA TOURNELLE

PONT DE LA TOURNELLE

Q. DE BÉTHUNE

PONT DE SULLY

RUE LAGRANGE

Place Maubert

MAUBERT-MUTUALITÉ

RUE DES BERNARDINS

PONTOISE

POISSY

BD SAINT-GERMAIN

ÉCOLES

RUE BEAUVAIS

3

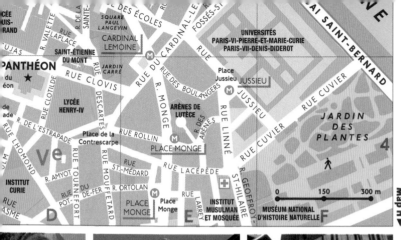

Map labels (partial, left-edge cut off):

DES ÉCOLES · SQUARE PAUL LANGEVIN · CARDINAL LEMOINE · SAINT-ÉTIENNE DU MONT · PANTHÉON · du éon · LYCÉE HENRY-IV · RUE CLOVIS · JARDIN CARRÉ · RUE DES BOULANGERS · Place Jussieu · JUSSIEU · UNIVERSITÉS PARIS-VI-PIERRE-ET-MARIE-CURIE PARIS-VII-DENIS-DIDEROT · QUAI SAINT-BERNARD · RUE CUVIER · JARDIN DES PLANTES · ARÈNES DE LUTÈCE · RUE LINNÉ · RUE CUVIER · Place de la Contrescarpe · PLACE MONGE · RUE LACÉPÈDE · INSTITUT CURIE · PLACE MONGE · Place Monge · INSTITUT MUSULMAN ET MOSQUÉE · MUSÉUM NATIONAL D'HISTOIRE NATURELLE · 0 150 300 m

ÉGLISE ST-SULPICE

ÉGLISE ST-GERMAIN-DES-PRÉS

...nding right next to the ...ains of the Gallo-Roman ...ns (1st–3rd c.), the Hôtel ...Abbés de Cluny (15th c.) ...e most magnificent ...mple of medieval ...sian non-religious ...itecture. The National ...seum of the Middle Ages ...ains a rich collection of ...cts. Its main attraction ...e famous 15th-century ...stry *Dame à la Licorne* *Lady and the Unicorn*).

...anthéon (A D4)
...du Panthéon (5th)
...10am–6.30pm
...1 Oct–March)
...by Louis XV, this
...ch was only completed
...89. Three years later

the Assembly dedicated it to the great names of the Revolution: Marat, Voltaire, Mirabeau and Rousseau. In 1885, it gained status as a mausoleum, in time to accept Victor Hugo's ashes.

★ Jardin du Luxembourg (A B3)
→ Daily 8am–sunset
Musée du Luxembourg
19, rue de Vaugirard (6th)
Tel 01 40 13 62 00
Fri–Mon 9am–10pm; Tue–Thu
10am–8pm
The avenues of horse chestnut trees, punctuated by an astonishing series of sculptures, the English garden and the Medici Fountain (1630) make this

the city's most romantic park. For over a century the ornamental lake has been a sailing ground for model-boat enthusiasts. Art exhibitions in the museum.

★ Église St-Sulpice (A B3)
→ Pl. St-Sulpice (6th)
Daily 7.30am–7.30pm
The construction of this enormous church lasted from 1646 to 1780. Its classic façade features three different architectural orders: Doric, Ionic and Corinthian. The interior too is on a monumental scale. Look out for the Chapel of the Angels, decorated with murals by Delacroix,

including his *Jacob Wrestling with the Angel* (1855–61).

★ Église St-Germain-des-Prés (A B2)
→ 3, pl. St-Germain-des-Prés (6th); Mon–Sat 8am–7.45pm; Sun 9am–8pm
The oldest church in Paris, built in AD990 on the foundations of a Merovingian basilica, which were uncovered in 1970. It has a 12th-century ambulatory clock tower and choir, ribbed vaulting in the 17th-century nave and 19th-century nave frescoes of scenes from the Old and New Testaments, including the admirable *Christ Entering Jerusalem* by Lattyre.

MUSÉE CARNAVALET

HÔTEL DE SOUBISE

MUSÉE PICASSO

★ **Les Halles (B** B2)
The Halles market had been feeding the French capital ever since the 12th century – Émile Zola was to call it 'the belly of Paris'. Massive works took place in the 1970s and the 'Forum' was created, a pedestrianized zone with a huge, partially underground shopping mall. Worth seeing are the Fountain of the Innocents (1549) and St Eustache (1532–1637), one of the few Renaissance churches in Paris. The Rue Montorgueil nearby is perhaps the last vestige of the old Halles, with market folk coming early to set up their stalls.

★ **Centre Georges-Pompidou (B** C3)
➔ *Rue St-Martin (4th)*
Museum: Wed–Mon 11am–9pm (10pm Thu)
A striking structure of glass, steel and plastic designed in 1971 by Richard Rogers, Renzo Piano and Gianfranco Franchini, Beaubourg – as it is also known – is a multi-discipline cultural center. Don't miss the Musée National d'Art Moderne, the second largest in the world, and go to the top floor for one of the best panoramic views of the city.

★ **Hôtel de Ville (B** C4)
➔ *Pl. de l'Hôtel-de-Ville (4th)*

Neo-Renaissance façade (1882) and an interior refurbished in the late 19th century, after the original building (1535) was destroyed by fire in 1871. The town hall contains an abundance of gilt, wood-paneling and Baccarat chandeliers, the spoils of the Third Republic. In winter the area in front is turned into a public skating rink.

★ **Maison Européenne de la Photographie (B** D4)
➔ *5-7, rue de Fourcy (4th)*
Tel. 01 44 78 75 00
Wed–Sun 11am–7.45pm
Important exhibitions of contemporary photography are held here in a fine

1706 town house.

★ **Place des Vosges (B** E
Maison Victor-Hugo
Tel 01 42 72 10 16
Tue–Sun 10am–6pm
Brick façades, high Fren gables, arcaded gallerie the sumptuous former Place Royale has retain all the splendor of the of Henry IV's reign. At n Victor Hugo's house is a small museum, whicl pays homage to the wr

★ **Hôtel de Sully (B** E
➔ *62, rue St-Antoine (4th*
Tel. 01 44 61 21 50
Mon–Fri 9am–5.30pm
One of the most elegar and impressive town houses in the Marais –

B

◀ **Map A**

LES HALLES

CENTRE GEORGES-POMPIDOU

HÔTEL DE VILLE

Les Halles / Le Marais

The ten iron-framed pavilions built by Victor Baltard for Napoleon III to house the markets have gone, and the Halles area, the center of modern Paris, is now famous for its vast shopping mall, the Forum. The Forum gardens, dotted with arcades and porticos, open out onto the church of St-Eustache. To the east, the Centre Pompidou, or Beaubourg, runs alongside the Stravinsky Fountain – a homage to the Russian musician. Further along, in the winding streets of the Marais, heavy doors hide splendid 17th-century town houses and a succession of Jewish stores, fashion boutiques and gay bars await visitors.

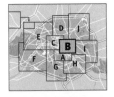

BISTROT BEAUBOURG

CHEZ MARIANNE

RESTAURANTS

Bistrot Beaubourg (B C3)
→ *25, rue Quincampoix (4th); Daily noon–2am*
A friendly, busy restaurant near the Pompidou Center serving simple but fresh and affordable food: andouillette, leeks in vinaigrette, etc. Entrées €6.40–12.

Marché des Enfants Rouges (B E2)
→ *39, rue de Bretagne (3rd); Tue-Sat 8am–1pm, 4-7.30pm (8pm Fri-Sat); Sun 8.30am–2pm*
The oldest food market in Paris (1615) has tables for you to eat some of the produce and freshly made dishes sold by its stalls – sushi, pizza, tajines, salads. Prix fixe €9–12.

Chez Marianne (B D3)
→ *2, rue des Hospitalières-St-Gervais (4th)*
Tel. 01 42 72 18 86
Daily 11am–midnight
A well-known deli specializing in Middle Eastern and East European Jewish food. The falafels, soused herring and pastrami can be eaten inside, on the terrace or taken out. Entrées €12–16.

Le Tambour (B B1)
→ *41, rue Montmartre (2nd)*
Tel. 01 42 33 06 90
Daily 7.30am–4am
A quirky bistro with a decor made of road signs, fire hydrants and retro métro maps. It feeds typical Parisian favorites to night owls, such as pigs' trotters, andouillette, ham with Puy lentils, etc. Entrées €12–22.

L'Ambassade d'Auvergne (B C2)
→ *22, rue du Grenier-St-Lazare (3rd)*
Tel. 01 42 72 31 22; Daily noon–2pm, 7.30–10pm
A long-established restaurant over several floors with a rustic decor. Serves specialties of the Auvergne and Aveyron regions, such as sausages with the famous *aligot* (mash with melted Tomme cheese and garlic). Prix fixe €20 (lunch), €28.

Chez Janou (B F3)
→ *2, rue Roger-Verlomme (3rd); Daily 7am–1am; kitchen open noon–3pm, 8pm–midnight*
A Provençal bistro behind the Place des Vosges with dishes from the south of France such as tuna carpaccio and sea bass with pesto. Service can be slow when the place gets busy (and it does), so relax with one of the 80 kinds of pastis on

ROGUERIE

FINKELSZTAJN

SENTOU

offer. Terrace. Prix fixe €13.50.Entrées €15–20.

Les Enfants Rouges (B E2)
→ 9, rue de Beauce (3rd)
Tel. 01 48 87 80 61
Wed-Sat noon–2.30pm,
7pm–midnight
A remarkable bistro: the cellar is stocked with rare but reasonably priced labels, and the food is delicate, with some Mediterranean accents. Prix fixe €17 (lunch), €34.

CAFÉS, BARS

L'Ébouillanté (B D4)
→ 6, rue des Barres (4th)
Tue-Sun noon–10.30pm
(7pm in winter)
Set in a pedestrianized street across from the church of St-Gervais-St-Protais. Ideal for lunch or tea on the terrace. Brunch on weekends.

Le Loir dans la Théière (B D3)
→ 3, rue des Rosiers (4th)
Daily 9am–7pm
Sink into the comfortable worn-out leather armchairs and linger in this warm, busy tearoom. Delicious homemade cakes, tarts and crumbles; salads at lunchtime.

Café Noir (B B1)
→ 65, rue Montmartre (2nd)
Mid-Oct-mid-April: Mon-Sat

9am (4pm Sat)–2am; mid-April-mid-Oct: daily 9am (4pm Sat-Sun)–2am
A friendly landlord, a splendid bar and outdoor terrace make this small café a very pleasant spot. Le Cœur Fou, at no. 55, is also worth a visit.

L'Art Brut (B C2)
→ 78, rue Quincampoix (3rd); Tel. 01 42 72 17 36
Daily 4pm–2am
The wrought-iron and wood decor, the sculptures and massive tables have turned this long, narrow place into a warm and friendly bar. Gypsy music, French songs, cheap beer and brandy from the Balkans.

La Gaîté Lyrique (B C1)
→ 3bis, rue Papin (3rd)
Tue-Sun 2–10pm (8pm Wed-Sat; 6pm Sun)
A 21st-century cultural space in a superb 19th-century theater; concerts, exhibitions, workshops, video games corner etc.

Rue des Lombards (B B3)
The home of jazz in Paris: mainstream, fusion, Afro, Latin and a whole lot more. Good places to try include the Duc des Lombards (no. 42), the Baiser Salé (no. 58) and Sunset-Sunside (no. 60).

SHOPPING

La Droguerie (B B2)
→ 9-11, rue du Jour (1st)
Tel. 01 45 08 93 27
Mon-Sat 2 (10.30am Tue-Sat)–6.45pm
A haberdashery store complete with countless jars of beads and ribbons of every hue.

Comptoir de la Gastronomie (B B2)
→ 34, rue Montmartre (1st)
Tel. 01 42 33 31 32; Mon 9am–11pm; Tue-Sat 6am–11pm (midnight Fri-Sat)
A store whose façade dates back to 1894, with foie gras, sausages, ham on the bone, pâtés and other delicacies. Some seating and good take-out sandwiches as well.

Finkelsztajn (B D3)
→ 27, rue des Rosiers (4th)
Tel. 01 42 72 78 91; Mon 11am–7pm; Wed-Sun 10am–7pm (7.30pm Fri-Sun)
The best Jewish-Askhenazi deli in Paris. Hummus, strudel, dill taramasalata, sernik (cheesecake) and bagels for royalty. Then if you like shopping, walk the Rue des Francs-Bourgeois, whose fashion shops are nearly all open on Sundays.

Sentou (B D4)
→ 29, rue François-Miron (4th); Tel. 01 42 78 50 60

Tue-Sat 10am–7pm
Three floors of trend-setting, colorful furniture and objects for the home by the latest designers: lights, vases, boxes, tables, for all budgets.

Izrael (B D4)
→ 30, rue François-Miron (4th); Tue-Fri 10.30am–1pm, 2–7pm; Sat 10am–7pm
Wonderful scents of exotic spices tickle your nostrils as soon as you enter this amazing store: tea from Mauritius, Indian curry, soap from Aleppo, as well as olives, rice, lentils and delicacies of all kinds.

Rue Étienne-Marcel (B B2)
This street and a few nearby (Rues du Jour, Tiquetonne, Montmartre) are lined with boutiques selling jewelry and fashion: Kabuki, Barbara Bui, Gas by Marie, Cop Copines, Saïki, Et Vous...

Mariage Frères (B D3)
→ 30, rue du Bourg-Tibourg (4th); Tel. 01 42 72 28 11
Daily 10.30am–7.30pm
Tearoom: daily noon–7pm
A magnificent colonial-style shop packed with some 500 varieties of tea. Tearoom as well.
And the **BHV (B** C3)
→ 52, rue de Rivoli (4th)
Small department store and mecca for DIY.

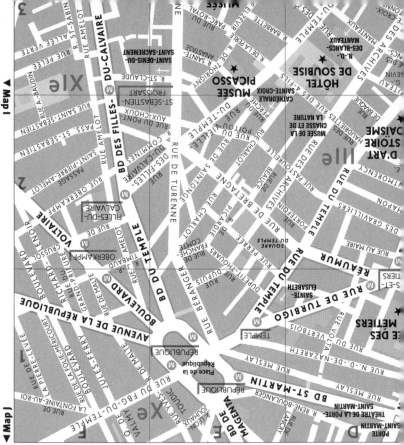

PLACE DES VOSGES

HÔTEL DE SULLY

ÉE D'ART ET D'HISTOIRE DU JUDAÏSME

MUSÉE DES ARTS ET MÉTIERS

center of society life
ng the time of the
es of Sully. The garden,
Renaissance main
tyard and the orangery
ill still intact. In the
r, note the bas-reliefs
cting the seasons.

tel

oubise (BD3)
, rue Francs-Bourgeois
: Tel. 01 40 27 60 96
 Wed-Fri 10am–12.30pm,
5pm; Sat-Sun 2–5.30pm
risian rocaille-style
erpiece built by
und in 1735. The
ere classical façade is
rk contrast to its
or, with extravagant
e-and-gold paneled

rooms and allegorical
stucco high-reliefs. The
building also houses the
National Archives and
exhibitions from the
Museum of French History.

**★ Musée
Carnavalet (B** E3)
→ 23, rue de Sévigné (3rd)
Tel. 01 44 59 58 58
Tue-Sun 10am–6pm
The Hôtel Carnavalet (16th
c.) and Hôtel Le Peletier de
St-Fargeau (17th c.) provide
the perfect setting for this
fascinating museum
devoted to the history of
Paris – its architecture,
society, culture, etc.

★ Musée Picasso (B E3)
→ 5, rue de Thorigny (3rd)

Tel. 01 42 71 25 21; Closed for
renovation until April 2013
The superb Hôtel Salé is
dedicated entirely to Pablo
Picasso (1881–1973),
whose works are viewed
chronologically, from his
earliest in Barcelona to his
final canvases painted in
Mougins. The quantity and
diversity of pieces makes
this the most important
collection of Picasso's
work in the world.

**★ Musée d'Art et
d'Histoire du Judaïsme
(B** D2)
→ 71, rue du Temple (3rd)
Tel. 01 53 01 86 60; Sun-Fri
11am (10am Sun)–6pm
A splendid 17th-century

town house, the Hôtel de
St-Aignan houses a
museum devoted to the
history of Jews in France,
their heritage and culture
through a collection of
manuscripts, liturgical
objects, works of art and
other memorabilia.

**★ Musée des Arts
et Métiers (B** D1)
→ 60, rue Réaumur (3rd)
Tel. 01 53 01 82 00; Tue-Sun
10am–6pm (9.30pm Thu)
On show here are Pascal's
calculating machine,
Lavoisier's laboratory,
Foucault's pendulum and
3,000 other technological
inventions from the 16th
century to the present day.

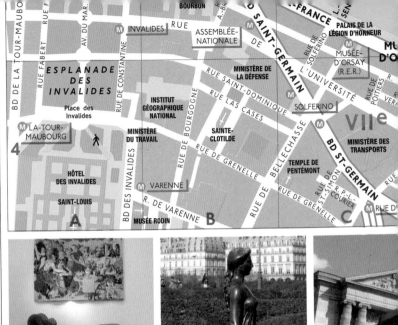

MUSÉE DES ARTS DÉCORATIFS

JARDINS DES TUILERIES

JEU DE PAUME

★ **Pinacothèque de Paris** (C C1)
→ 28, pl. de la Madeleine (8th); Daily 10.30am–6.30pm (9pm Wed & Fri)
Open since 2007 on the Place de la Madeleine, it is run privately and houses art exhibitions of all kinds.

★ **Opéra Garnier** (C D1)
→ Tel. 01 40 01 17 89
Tours: daily 10am–5.30pm (4.30pm mid-Sep to mid-July)
This grand Second Empire building designed by Charles Garnier in 1874, and dedicated to 'art, luxury and pleasure', is a blend of neo-Renaissance and baroque styles. Antique masks and statues

of composers decorate the façade. Inside, the two-flight staircase leads to the red-and-gold room, under a ceiling painted by Chagall, and to sumptuous halls with a decor of frescoes and mosaics. Opera and dance performances.

★ **Place Vendôme** (C D2)
Superb yet austere, this square, inaugurated in 1699 and built in the shape of a rectangle with its corners cut off, was originally a virtually enclosed space measuring 160 by 150 yards. In the center is the Vendôme column (19th century), made famous by Napoleon.

Hidden behind the 80-ft-high walls are magnificent town houses, one of which is the Hôtel Ritz (no. 15).

★ **Palais-Royal** (C E2)
→ Pl. du Palais-Royal (2nd)
It was under these now peaceful arcades that Parisian commerce spread in 1780, as did gambling and prostitution, while ideas of a revolution were beginning to circulate in the clubs. Home to Cardinal Richelieu, then to the dukes of Orléans, the palace now houses the Constitutional Council, the State Council and the Ministry of Culture, which overlooks the main courtyard, redesigned

by Buren in 1986.

★ **Musée du Louvre** (C
→ Cour Napoléon (1st)
Tel. 01 40 20 50 50; Wed-M 9am–6pm (9.45pm Wed &
The most visited museu in the world, entered vi Ieoh Ming Pei's glass pyramid (1988), has ov 30,000 works of art displayed over 200,00 ft. Formerly a royal pala the Louvre opened to th public in 1793. In the m of rooms, from the Mid Ages to the 19th centur from Egyptian antiquiti to European paintings, Venus de Milo, The Raft c Medusa and the Mona L are still stealing the sh

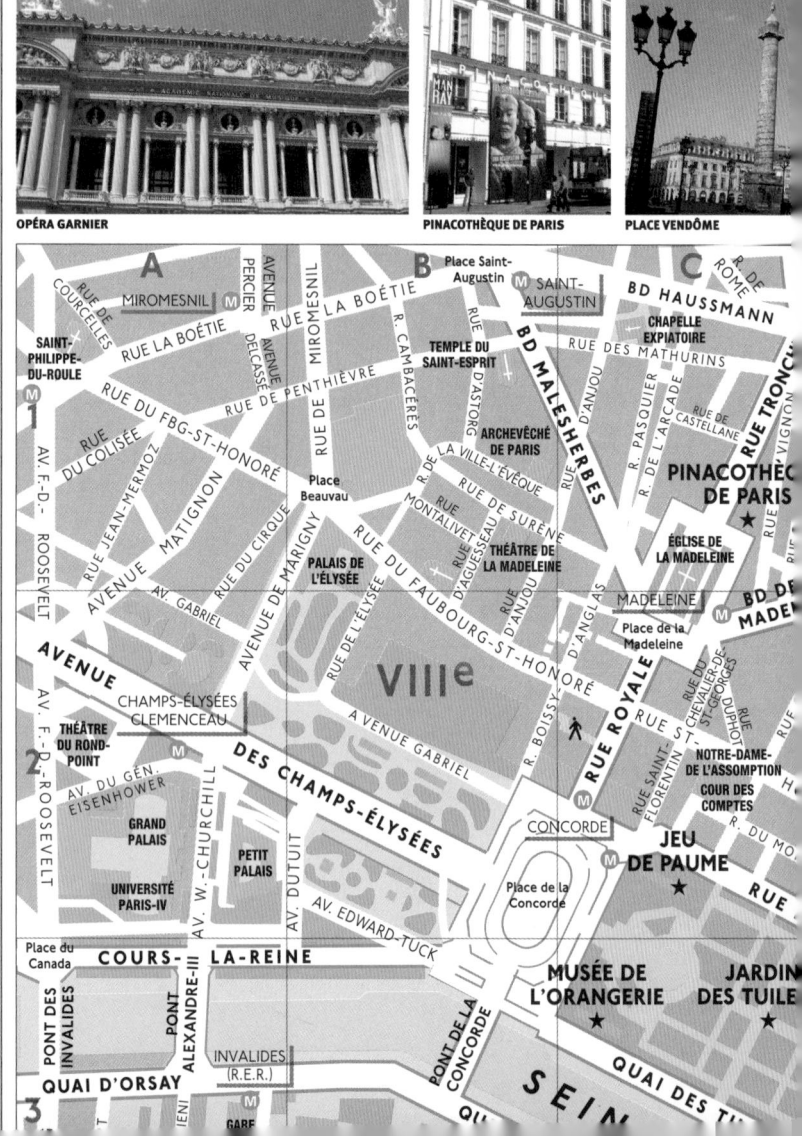

OPÉRA GARNIER

PINACOTHÈQUE DE PARIS

PLACE VENDÔME

▲ Map E

Facing one another across the river, the city's two greatest museums, the Louvre and Orsay, are firm favorites with tourists. Although the souvenir stores have invaded the arcades along the Rue de Rivoli, the area has lost none of its grandeur. Place de la Madeleine and the Rue Royale boast a number of designer tableware shops and luxurious delis; fashion designers line Rue St-Honoré, and Place Vendôme is home to some of the most famous jewelry names in the world. To escape the uproar of the streets head for the peaceful gardens of the Palais Royal, or its pleasant tearooms and elegant restaurants.

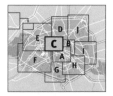

HIGUMA

LE GRAND VÉFOUR

RESTAURANTS

Higuma (C E2)
→ *32bis, rue Ste-Anne (1st)*
Daily 11.30am–10pm
In a street famous for its canteen-style Japanese eateries. Diners eat at large formica tables while the chefs prepare ramen (noodle soup) and other specialties in sizzling woks. Also at 163, rue St-Honoré (**C** E3). Prix fixe €10–12; entrées €6–9.

Olio Pane Vino (C F3)
→ *44, rue Coquillère (1st)*
Tel. 01 42 33 21 15
Tue-Wed noon–2.15pm;
Thu-Sat noon–2.30pm,
8–10.30pm
There's more than just oil, bread and wine to be had in this Italian grocery-cum-trattoria, which sells and serves delicious antipasti, pasta, quality charcuterie and outstanding desserts. Entrées €13–18.

Juveniles (C E2)
→ *47, rue de Richelieu (1st)*
Tel. 01 42 97 46 49; Mon-Sat 6 (noon Tue-Sat)–11pm
A renowned wine bar with only a dozen tables where Tim Johnston sells the fine vintages he's sourced from all over the world. Pleasant atmosphere and good, simple cuisine and tapas.

Prix fixe €16.50; entrées €15–18. Try also Willi's Wine Bar around the corner (*13, rue des Petits Champs*, **C** E2).

Aux Lyonnais (C E1)
→ *32, rue St-Marc (2nd)*
Tel. 01 42 96 65 04
Tue-Fri noon–2pm, 7.30–10.30pm; Sat 7.30–10.30pm
Alain Ducasse's bistro, in a splendid building dating from the end of the 19th century, specializes in Lyonnaise cuisine. Ancient recipes are revived for epicureans: egg cocotte with crayfish, veal liver with parsley. Traditional and heart warming. Entrées €16–30; prix fixe €30 (lunch).

L'Absinthe (C D2)
→ *24, pl. du Marché-St-Honoré (1st); Tel. 01 49 26 90 04; Mon-Fri 12.15–2.15pm, 7.15–10.30pm; Sat 7.15–11pm*
A smart Parisian spot with a fine terrace on a lively pedestrian square. Haute bistro cuisine with a thoroughly enjoyable seasonal menu. Entrées €22; prix fixe €31, €39.

Le Grand Véfour (C E2)
→ *17, rue de Beaujolais (1st)*
Tel. 01 42 96 56 27; Mon-Fri 12.30–1.45pm, 8–9.45pm
One of the oldest and most stunning

CAFÉ MARLY

COLETTE

FIFI CHACHNIL

restaurants in Paris, set under the Palais-Royal arcades, with a listed decor, plush banquettes and three Michelin stars. Don't miss Guy Martin's now classic truffle flavored foie gras raviolis. Reservations essential. Prix fixe €96 (lunch), €282; entrées €85–102.

CAFÉS, BARS, CLUB

Le Café Marly (C E3)
→ *93, rue de Rivoli (1st)*
Daily 8am–2am
This stylish café overlooks the glass pyramid and French sculpture rooms of the Louvre. Coffee may be pricey, but the views are majestic.
Angelina (C D3)
→ *226, rue de Rivoli (1st)*
Tel. 01 42 60 82 00
Daily 7.30am (8.30am Sat-Sun)–7pm
Opened in 1903 under the arcades of Rue de Rivoli, this Viennese tearoom serves one of the best hot chocolates in Paris, brought to you on a silver tray with a cup of Chantilly cream. It can also be taken out.
Bar de l'Entracte (C E2)
→ *47, rue de Montpensier (1st); Mon-Sat 9am–1.30am; Sun 10am–8pm*
A historic, attractive café

next to the Comédie-Française and Palais-Royal theaters, where actors and spectators alike share a pre- or post-show drink.
93 Montmartre (C F2)
→ *93, rue Montmartre (2nd)*
Tel. 01 40 28 02 83
Mon-Sat 9am–2am
A bar-restaurant, all velvet curtains and Chesterfield couches, where a hip set comes to eat (until midnight) and dance.
Legrand Filles et Fils (C F2)
→ *1, rue de la Banque (1st)*
Tel. 01 42 60 07 12
Mon-Sat noon–9pm
On one side, a gorgeous 1900 *épicerie* selling fine preserves, jams, biscuits and sweets. On the other, a wine shop that leads onto the magnificent Galerie Vivienne. Sit down around the bar for a plate of charcuterie and a glass of red wine (*daily noon–7pm*). Exceptional labels.
Social Club (C F2)
→ *142, rue Montmartre (2nd); Tel. 01 40 28 05 55 Wed-Sat 11pm–6am*
Arguably the hottest spot on the Paris club scene: electro DJ as well as dubstep or hip hop. In the basement is Le Silencio, designed by David Lynch.

THEATER

Comédie-Française (C E3)
→ *Pl. Colette (1st)*
Tel. 08 25 10 16 80 (box office); Daily 11am–6pm
The French national theater, founded in 1680, has been in the Salle Richelieu at the Palais Royal since 1799.

SHOPPING

Repetto (C D2)
→ *22, rue de la Paix (2nd)*
Mon-Sat 9.30am–7.30pm
A legendary boutique well known by Opéra dancers and brought up to date by Issey Miyake. His ballet shoes come in an amazing range of colors and materials.
The arcades of the Palais-Royal (C E2-3)
The beautiful, romantic arcades around the garden are lined with high-fashion as well as old-fashioned boutiques.
Les Salons Shiseido
→ *142, gal. de Valois (1st)*
Tel. 01 49 27 09 09
Mon-Sat 10am–7pm
The exotic perfumes created by Serge Lutens for Shiseido are sold exclusively in this store.
Didier Ludot
→ *24, gal. de Montpensier*

(1st); Tel. 01 42 96 06 56 Mon-Sat 11am–7pm
Forty years of past Chanel and Dior creations hang in this treasure trove. Visit Ludot's other shop (125, gal. de Valois) for that special little black number.
Anna Joliet
→ *9, rue de Beaujolais (1st)*
Mon-Sat 10.30am–7pm
A doll's-house style stall selling pretty music boxes.
Colette (C D2)
→ *213, rue St-Honoré (1st)*
Tel. 01 55 35 33 90
Mon-Sat 11am–7pm
The very latest in fashion, art and design: streetwear, CDs, books and stage costumes. Waterbar and food available downstairs.
Fifi Chachnil (C D2)
→ *231, rue St-Honoré (1st)*
Tel. 01 42 61 21 83
Mon-Sat 11am–7pm
Glamorous, sexy lingerie in bright colors for women of the 21st century.
Françoise Montague (C D2)
→ *231, rue St-Honoré (1st)*
Tel. 01 42 61 21 83
Mon-Sat 10.30am (11.30am Sat)–7pm
Finely crafted jewelry, including the famous flower rings and Swarovski crystal bracelets. Items can also be made to order.

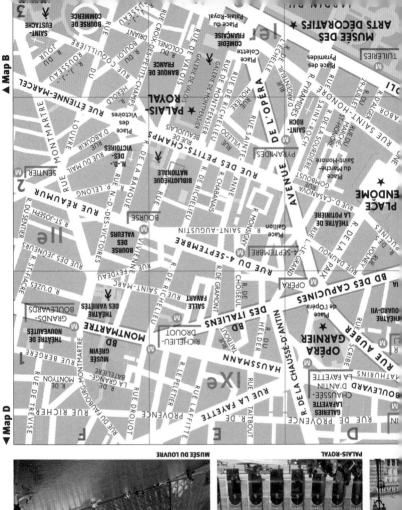

MUSÉE DU LOUVRE

PALAIS-ROYAL

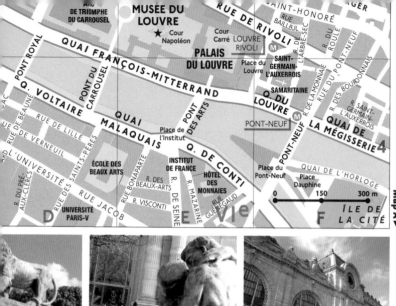

MUSÉE DE L'ORANGERIE

MUSÉE D'ORSAY

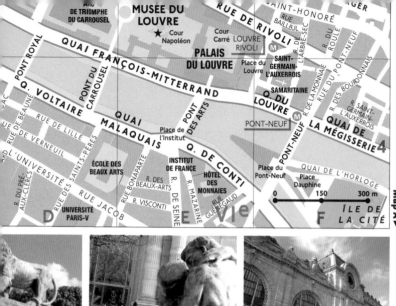

Map A ▶

ÎLE DE
LA CITÉ

usée des Arts
oratifs (C D3)

7, rue de Rivoli (1st)
1 44 55 57 50; Tue-Sun
–6pm (9pm Thu)
sed in a wing of the
re, it presents a unique
ction of furniture and
ts d'art from the
lles Ages to the present
Look out for sections
ted to fashion and
es, and to advertising.
modern bar-restaurant
a fabulous terrace
ing onto the Tuileries.

rdins
Tuileries (C C3)

du Carrousel (1st); June-
daily 7am–11pm; Sep-
h: daily 7.30am–7.30pm;

April-May: daily 7am–9pm
In 1666, Le Nôtre
transformed the park of the
Château des Tuileries into
a French-style garden and
opened up the view to the
west with a road which
later became the Champs-
Élysées. The two lakes, the
terraces running along the
Seine and the Rue de
Rivoli, the many chestnut
and lime trees growing on
either side of the central
avenue all convey the
romance of times past.

★ **Jeu de Paume (C** C2)
→ *1, pl. de la Concorde (8th)*
Tel. 01 47 03 12 50;
Tue-Fri noon–7pm (9pm Tue);
Sat-Sun 10am–7pm

The former Jeu de Paume,
built for Napoleon III in
1862, has been used for
exhibitions of contemporary
art since 1922. After the
latest restoration in 2004,
it now mounts photography,
video, film and new media
exhibitions.

★ **Musée
de l'Orangerie (C** C3)
→ *Tel. 01 44 77 80 07*
Wed-Mon 9am–6pm
One of a pair with the Jeu
de Paume, the Orangerie
(1852) displays the
marvelous series of
Waterlilies presented by
Monet in 1922. In the
basement is the Walter-
Guillaume collection of

modern art: 144 works by
Cézanne, Matisse, Picasso,
Modigliani and others.

★ **Musée d'Orsay (C** C4)
→ *1, rue de Bellechasse (7th)*
Tel. 01 40 49 48 14; Tue-Sun
9.30am–6pm (9.45pm Thu)
Painting and sculptures
from the 19th and early
20th centuries are displayed
under the impressive glass
roof of the former Orléans
railway station (1900).
Converted into a museum
in 1977–86, this temple of
Impressionism shows
works by the most brilliant
artists of the period: Degas,
Manet, Gauguin, Van Gogh,
Renoir, etc. Significant
retrospectives. Great café.

MUSÉE DE MONTMARTRE

CIMETIÈRE DE MONTMARTRE

D

★ **Sacré-Cœur (D** C3)
→ *Tel. 01 53 41 89 00*
Daily 9am–10.30pm
Built during the tumultuous period of the 1870 defeat against the Prussians and the Commune, the basilica was the result of the National Vow made in 1873 to atone for the lack of religious faith typical of the century – and supposed to be the origin of the country's misfortunes. A symbol of the Butte, this church, with its white Romanesque-Byzantine silhouette, attracts thousands of tourists each year. There are impressive mosaics inside the

basilica, and you can get an exhilarating view of the capital from the esplanade and the dome.
★ **Église St-Pierre-de-Montmartre (D** C3)
→ *2, rue du Mont-Cenis (18th)*
Daily 9am–7pm
One of the oldest churches in Paris, hidden behind an 18th-century façade. This is all that now remains of the Abbaye aux Dames (1147), erected on what is thought to be the site of an ancient Gallo-Roman temple.
★ **Place du Tertre (D** C3)
Street artists specializing in portraits or caricatures, cafés, flocks of tourists... this former square of the

old village has become a Montmartre cliché. But in the early morning when the square is at its quietest, it is still very pleasant to have coffee on the terrace of La Mère Catherine, a bistro opened in 1789.
★ **Musée de Montmartre (D** C3)
→ *12, rue Cortot (18th)*
Tel. 01 49 25 89 39
Daily 10am–6pm
Housed in a pretty 18th-century folly overlooking the vineyards, this museum tells the complete history of the area via paintings, photographs, music and posters.

★ **Cimetière de Montmartre (D** A3)
→ *20, av. Rachel (18th)*
Mid-March-Oct: daily 8am (8.30am Sat; 9am Sun)–6
Nov-mid-March: daily 8am (9am Sun)–5.30pm
The undulating countryside, the 100-year-old trees and the beautiful statues all contrive to make this cemetery truly romantic. Here lie the remains of, among others, Dumas, Stendhal, Vigny, Berlioz, Offenbach, Fragonard, Degas, Guitry, Nijinsky, Truffaut, the singer Dalida as well as those of well-known local characters such as the great illust

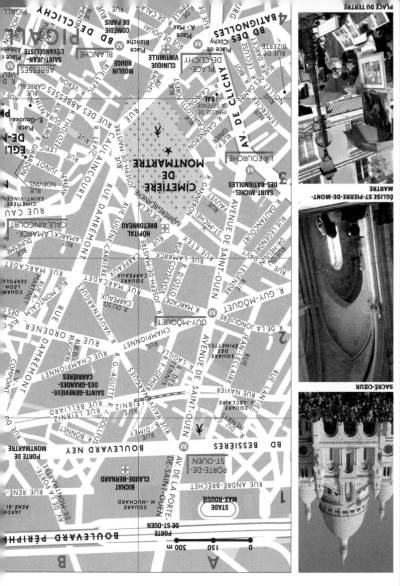

PLACE DU TERTRE

ÉGLISE ST-PIERRE-DE-MONT-
MARTRE

SACRÉ-CŒUR

High above the Abbesses district and its trendy bars, the dazzling white domes and bell towers of the Sacré-Cœur Basilica draw the eye. The artists, cabarets and balls of the Belle Époque may be long gone but the charm of Montmartre lives on in the steep streets, flights of steps and ivy-covered houses. On the boulevards at the foot of the Butte (mound) Montmartre, the concert halls fill up as evening falls, while the sex scene in Pigalle begins to come to life. Nearby, the 'Nouvelle Athènes' (New Athens) entices visitors with its romantic streets lined with town houses built int he 1820s – an oasis before the bustle of the big boulevards.

BOUILLON CHARTIER

LA FAMILLE

RESTAURANTS

Au Bon Coin (D B2)
→ 49, rue des Cloÿs (18th)
Tel. 01 46 06 91 36
Mon-Sat 8am–midnight
(9pm Sat); kitchen: Mon-Thu
noon–2pm, 7–10.30pm
On the far side of the Butte, away from the crowds, is a classic Parisian bistro with wines by the glass, charcuterie and brasserie-style meals. Deli and art gallery too. Entrées €8–13.

Les Pâtes Vivantes (D C6)
→ 46, rue du Fbg-Montmartre (9th)
Tel. 01 45 23 10 21; Mon-Sat noon–3pm, 7–11pm
A steamy, bustling Chinese cafeteria where fresh noodles (hence the name, 'noodles alive') are kneaded, stretched and hand-rolled in front of customers, then thrown into a bowl of soup with chicken, beef, tofu... Entrées €9.50–14.50.

Bouillon Chartier (D C6)
→ 7, rue du Fbg-Montmartre (9th); Tel. 01 47 70 86 29
Daily 11.30am–10pm
A magnificent Belle Époque 'soup kitchen' and the first of its kind when it opened in 1896. It is touristy, the food is simple classic French –

leeks in vinaigrette, beef bourguignonne – but it's fun. Entrées €10–14.

Le BAL Café (D A4)
→ 6, impasse de la Défense (18th); Tel 01 44 70 75 51
Wed-Sun 10am–11pm (7pm Sun); brunch: Sat-Sun 11.30am–4pm
A new-wave café where two young chefs prepare a new British food menu. When you've tucked into a pie or oxtail stew with Guinness, have a look at one of the exhibitions: BAL is an arts center displaying photographs and short movies. Entrées €14.50–17. Prix fixe €11 (lunch), €30.

Pooja (D D6)
→ 91, passage Brady (10th)
Tel. 01 48 24 00 83; Daily noon–2.30pm, 6.30–11pm
The covered arcade called the Passage Brady is a little Indian ghetto, and just the place to try some fine North Indian food, served outside beneath the glass roof. Entrées €12–14.50; prix fixe €12 (lunch), €17.50, €25.

La Famille (D C4)
→ 41, rue des Trois-Frères (18th); Tel. 01 42 52 11 12
Tue-Sat 8pm–2am (kitchen closes 11.15pm)
A small restaurant with a bare decor but warm atmosphere, and a

AN DU MONDE   HORTENSIA LOUISOR   À LA MÈRE DE FAMILLE

stunningly creative cuisine by Jaume Moreira. The seasonal menu changes every two weeks and many dishes boast a sweet-and-sour flavor – pan-fried squid, foie gras ravioli, tuna steak with dried fruit and polenta. Attractive bar for a post-dinner cocktail. Reserve. Prix fixe €31–50.

CAFÉS, BARS, CLUBS, CONCERTS

Au Rendez-vous des Amis (D C4)
➔ 23, rue Gabrielle (18th)
Daily 8am-1.30am
A small, friendly café on the Butte but off the tourist track, with plenty of locals and a youthful ambience.
Le Sancerre (D B4)
➔ 35, rue des Abbesses (18th); Tel. 01 42 58 08 20
Daily 7am-2am
A compulsory stop if you are in the Abbesses district, this café-bar is at its best in the late afternoon and evening, when the large terrace is inundated with locals.
L'Olympic Café (D D3)
➔ 20, rue Léon (18th)
Tel. 01 42 52 29 93
Tue-Sat 5pm-2am
A large, lively bar in the Goutte-d'Or area, with a

mixed, bohemian crowd. The vast room downstairs stages a wide variety of concerts with jazz, gypsy, reggae and African music.
La Fourmi (D B4)
➔ 74, rue des Martyrs (18th)
Tel. 01 42 64 70 35
Mon-Sat 8am-2am (4am Fri-Sat); Sun 10am-2am
A few yards from the famous concert hall La Cigale, the trendy Fourmi attracts the bright young crowd of the 18th arrondissement for coffee, salad or late drinks.
Prix fixe €9.70.
Divan du Monde (D B4)
➔ 75, rue des Martyrs (18th)
Tel. 01 42 52 02 46
divandumonde.com
One of the best of its kind, this is a club, a very pleasant bar and a concert venue with an eclectic program of indie rock, punk, hip hop, new wave and fusion electro.
Rex Club (D C6)
➔ 5, bd Poissonnière (2nd)
Tel. 01 42 36 10 96
Wed-Sat 11.30pm-6am
The Grands Boulevards have been given a new lease of nightlife thanks to places like the Rex, which, for more than 20 years, has been one of the city's most important venues for electronic music. The noise is

deafening, with some of the best DJs in the world.
Le Pompon (D D6)
➔ 39, rue des Petites-Ecuries (10th); Tel. 01 53 34 60 85; Mon-Sat 7pm-2am
A synagogue converted into a trendy bar which has already become a cult, thanks to the barman's way with cocktails. Downstairs is a dance floor that gets packed at weekends.

SHOPPING

Anouschka (D A5)
➔ 6, av. du Coq (9th)
Tel. 01 48 74 37 00
Mon-Fri noon-7pm by appt
Former model turned stylist, Anouschka has organized her vintage finds chronologically, all by well-known designers.
Hortensia Louisor (D B5)
➔ 14, rue Clauzel (9th)
Tel. 01 45 26 67 68
Mon 2.30-7pm;
Tue-Sat 11.30am-7.30pm
Original clothes by two sisters. Their chic and affordable range fits all sizes, for women aged 20 upward.
À la Mère de Famille (D C6)
➔ 35, rue du Fbg-Montmartre (9th); Tel. 01 47 70 83 69; Mon-Sat 9.30am-

8pm; Sun 10am-1pm
One of the last of its kind, this beautiful, old-fashioned candy shop established in 1761 sells jams, sweets and candy: lollipops, calissons (sugar-coated almond paste), marrons glacés (candied chestnuts), etc.
Petit Pan (D C4)
➔ 10bis, rue Yvonne Le Tac (18th); Tel. 01 42 23 63 78
Daily 10.30am-7.30pm
Gorgeous mobiles, delicate silk paper kites and colorful pajamas for children, all from China. Also 76, rue F.-Miron (**B** D4), 95, rue du Bac (**G** B1), 7, rue de Prague (**I** B3).
Marché St-Pierre (D C4)
➔ 2, rue Charles-Nodier (18th); Tel. 01 46 06 92 25
Mon-Sat 10am-6.30pm (7pm Sat)
Truly the best place to buy fabric, it has attracted sewing enthusiasts, designers and interior decorators for decades.
Rue des Gardes (D D3)
In the Goutte-d'Or is a street lined with rooms of 12 young and vibrant designers. Look out for the clothes of designer Sakina M'sa at no. 6.
Also, the department stores **Printemps** and **Galeries Lafayette** (**D** A6).

▲ Map J

MUSÉE GUSTAVE-MOREAU

NOUVELLE ATHÈNES

HALLE ST-PIERRE

COVERED PASSAGEWAYS

MUSÉE GRÉVIN

Map B ▶

...bot and the French
...can dancer La Goule.
...alle St-Pierre (**D** C4)
→ *rue Ronsard (18th)*
1 42 58 72 89
...uly: Mon-Sat 10am–6pm
Sat); Sun 11am–6pm;
Mon-Fri noon–6pm
...glass and iron-covered
...cetplace (1868) houses
...Max-Fourny collection
...ive art, as well as a
...ry dedicated to
...lar contemporary art
...all over the world.
...ialist library and
...sant tearoom.

...uvelle
...nes (**D** B5)
...onstruction of the
...gle formed by Place

Pigalle/Notre-Dame-de-
Lorette/Ste-Trinité started
in 1820. The place is full of
romantic splendor: vaulted
passageways, neoclassical
buildings, English gardens,
where a community of
artists, such as Berlioz,
Sand, Degas, Chopin and
Dumas, once lived and
worked. Around the lovely
Square St-Georges,
the slightly more recent
façades (1830s) feature
neo-Renaissance patterns.
★ Musée Gustave-
Moreau (**D** B5)
→ *14, rue de La*
Rochefoucauld (9th)
Tel. 01 48 74 38 50; Mon, Wed-
Thu, 10am–12.45pm, 2–5pm;

Fri-Sun 10am–5pm
One of the prettiest small
museums in Paris. Around
5,000 drawings and 1,200
paintings by the symbolist
painter Gustave Moreau
(1826–98), including
Jupiter et Sémélé, are on
show in his former mansion-
studio, which was turned
into a museum in 1903.
Also look out for the
Museum of Romanticism,
at 16, rue Chaptal (**D** B4).
★ Covered
passageways (**D** C6)
→ *10-11 bd Montmartre (2nd)*
It took architectural sleight
of hand to build this
superb series of *passages
couverts*, glass-covered

passageways, and conceal
the irregularities of the site.
The Panoramas walkway
opened in 1799, followed
by Jouffroy and Verdeau in
1846 and 1847. Some of
the shop windows are
almost miniature museums,
filled with books, toys, etc.
★ Musée Grévin (**D** C6)
→ *10, bd Montmartre (9th)*
Tel. 01 47 70 85 05; Mon-Fri
10am–6.30pm; Sat-Sun
9.30am–7pm
This museum was opened
in 1881 by journalist Arthur
Meyer and caricaturist
Alfred Grévin. It contains
hundreds of celebrities and
influential figures
immortalized as waxworks.

MUSÉE JACQUEMART-ANDRÉ

MUSÉE NISSIM-DE-CAMONDO

PARC MONCEAU

★ Place de la Concorde (E F4)

This busy crossroads is also one of the most exquisite spots in Paris, designed for Louis XV in 1754. Contrary to other royal squares it is only walled on one side in order to maintain the perspective of the triumphal axis: to the east are the Tuileries and the Louvre Palace; to the west, the Champs-Élysées. Around the square are 18 rostral columns designed by Hittorff (1830). At its center, erected in 1836, is the Luxor Obelisk presented by the viceroy of Egypt.

★ Petit Palais (E E4)

→ Av. Winston-Churchill (8th)
Tel. 01 53 43 40 00
Tue-Sun 10am–6pm
The flamboyant gilded building houses the City of Paris Museum of Fine Arts, a collection extending from antiquity up to the Belle Époque, with a large section devoted to 19th-century French painting.

★ Grand Palais (E E4)

→ 3 av. du Gal Eisenhower (8th); Tel. 01 44 13 17 30
Exhibitions: Wed-Mon 10am–8pm (10pm Wed)
One of the most important buildings to be erected for the 1900 Exhibition, with the nearby Petit Palais and Pont Alexandre-III. The sublime glass-roofed hall hosts some of the city's most popular exhibitions. Its Art Nouveau cupola, framed by 9,370 tons of green steel, is an absolute beauty. The rear wing houses the Palais de la Découverte, a science museum with fascinating interactive displays for children. The bar-restaurant has a splendid terrace.

★ Arc de Triomphe (E C3)

→ Pl. Charles-de-Gaulle (8th)
Daily 10am–11pm (10.30pm Oct-March)
Symbol of the Napoleonic era, this huge neoclassical triumphal arch (1836) displays the art of the greatest sculptors working in the first half of the 19th century. You have to get very close to the *Marseillaise* by Rude (on the Champs-Élysées side) to feel the sheer power of it. There are magnificent views of the aptly named star-shaped esplanade (Place de l'Étoile) from the top of the arch. Under it is the tomb of the *Unknown Soldier* (1920).

★ La Défense (E A1)

A business district bristling with skyscrapers that began to appear in the 1960s, extending west for 4 miles, the axis going from Place de la Concorde to the Étoile. Its key fea

E

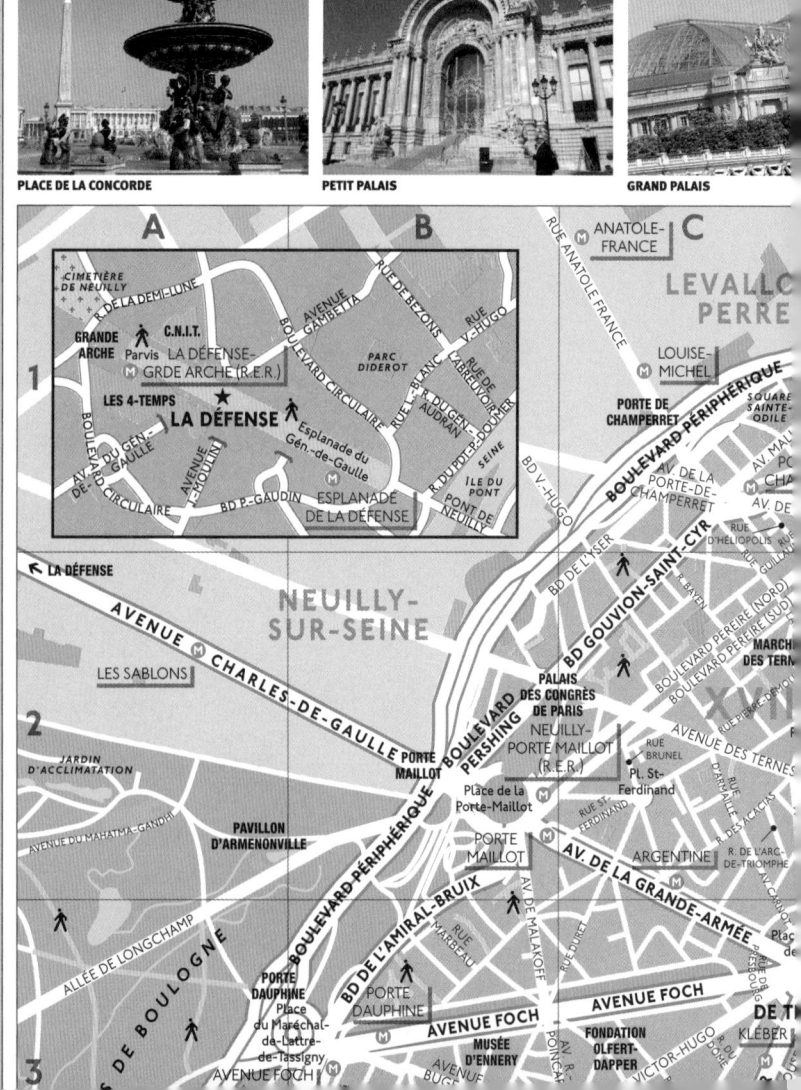

PLACE DE LA CONCORDE

PETIT PALAIS

GRAND PALAIS

Stretching majestically from La Concorde to the Arc de Triomphe the Champs-Élysées is an unforgettable sight, especially in December when the Christmas lights are on. The movie theaters, restaurants, boutiques and exclusive clubs lining the famous avenue draw a colorful crowd day and night. To the south stand the Petit and Grand Palais, with the Alexandre III bridge (1900) beyond, surmounted by golden winged horses. To the north is the featureless but well-heeled 17th arrondissement, with the stunning Parc Monceau. The district recovers some of the city's bohemian spirit in the old working-class district of Batignolles.

ATAO, LA DAME AUX HUÎTRES

CAFÉ JACQUEMART-ANDRÉ

RESTAURANTS

Comptoir de l'Arc (E D3)
→ 73, av. Marceau (8th)
Mon-Fri 7am-1am
A large and fashionable café whose terrace is always packed, and a useful place to eat near the Étoile without going over budget. Brasserie-style food. Entrées €9-15.

Atao, la Dame aux Huîtres (E F1)
→ 86, rue Lemercier (17th)
Tel. 01 46 27 81 12; Tue-Sat noon-3pm, 7-midnight; Sun noon-midnight
A good place for a break after visiting Batignolles market. Shellfish and oysters arrive daily from Brittany. The lady here also sells boxes to take out. Prix fixe €20 (lunch); entrées €18-26.

La Maison de l'Aubrac (E D3)
→ 37, rue Marbeuf (8th)
Tel. 01 43 59 05 14
Daily, 24 hrs
'From the pitchfork to the fork' is the restaurant's motto here. It specializes in beef, and the meat comes directly from owner Christian Valette's family farm. Traditional cuisine from the Aveyron region and a splendid wine list. Friendly atmosphere and a jovial clientele. Entrées

€12-40.

Relais de Venise – L'Entrecôte (E B2)
→ 271, Bd Pereire (17th)
Tel. 01 45 74 27 97; Daily noon-2.30pm, 7-11.45pm
A brasserie next door to the Palais des Congrès, which since 1959 has been serving only one dish: a juicy sirloin steak with matchstick fries and their own secret sauce. There's no booking: come either early or late if you don't want to wait. Entrées €26.

Le Bistral (E F1)
→ 80, rue Lemercier (17th)
Tel. 01 42 63 59 61; Tue-Sat noon-2.30pm, 8-1am
A long, thin dining room in which to try a seriously good, imaginative regional cuisine, with some unusual desserts. Good wine list. Pricey but first class. Prix fixe €29, €58; entrées €20-26.

L'Évasion (E F3)
→ 7, pl. St-Augustin (8th)
Tel. 01 45 22 66 20
Mon-Fri noon-2.30pm, 7.30-10.30pm
Wooden tables, chalkboards on the wall and the hushed tones of gourmets hard at work, savoring each dish. This smart bistro serves meat of exceptional quality and has an outstanding wine list too. Entrées €28-40.

WCASE

LADURÉE

BATIGNOLLES ORGANIC MARKET

TEAROOMS, CAFÉS

La Pâtisserie par V. Mauclerc (E D2)
→ 11, rue Poncelet (17th)
Tel. 01 42 27 81 83
Tue-Sat 9am–7.30pm;
Sun 9am–1.30pm
Poppy-seed cake with cherries, Sachertorte and other confections are served upstairs in an attractive tearoom or out on the terrace. Substantial dishes, such as beef strudel, are available at lunchtime.

Café Jacquemart-André (E E3)
→ 158, bd Haussmann (8th)
Tel. 01 45 62 11 59
Mon-Fri 11.45am–7pm (5.30pm Tue-Fri); Sat-Sun 11am–7pm (5.30pm Sun); tearoom from 3pm
The elegant tearoom of the Jacquemart-André Museum, where you can relax beneath a ceiling painted by Tiepolo or have brunch on the terrace overlooking the garden.

Pasteleria Belém (E F1)
→ 47, rue Boursault (17th)
Tel. 01 45 22 38 95
Tue-Sun 8am–8pm
An authentic Lisbon pâtisserie decorated with azulejos, and with only five tables. The pastel de nata (small custard tart) is not to be missed.

3 Pièces Cuisine (E F2)
→ 101, rue des Dames (17th)
Tel 01 44 90 85 10;
Daily 8am (9.30am Sat-Sun)–1.30am
A friendly local café opening onto the Rue des Dames. A few good value, restorative dishes are available, which explains the number of students at lunchtime. The place gets rowdier in the evening.

BAR, CLUBS

Flûte (E D2)
→ 19, rue de l'Étoile (17th)
Tel. 01 45 72 10 14
Tue-Fri 5pm–2am
A narrow champagne bar with a red speakeasy decor, where you can sit with a glass of fizz (there are over 100 labels to choose from) for as long as you want, listening to music imported daily from the Big Apple. Happy hour (Tue 5–8pm); live jazz (Wed evenings).

Showcase (E E4)
→ Pont Alexandre-III, Cours La-Reine (8th)
Tel. 01 45 61 25 43
Fri-Sat 11.30pm–6am
A concert venue and club in a former boathouse beneath the Alexandre III bridge. One of the coolest nightspots on the Right Bank, with live bands and

the latest techno sounds.

Chez Raspoutine (E D3)
→ 58, rue de Bassano (8th)
Tel 01 47 20 04 31
Tue-Sat 11pm–5am
A glitzy Russian cabaret, gloriously kitsch, which is now a club for the gilded youth of Paris specializing in DJ electro. Wearing a chapka or a fur coat may help you get in!

Queen (E D3)
→ 102, av. des Champs-Élysées (8th)
Tel. 08 92 70 73 30
Daily, 11.30pm (midnight Tue, Sun)–6am; queen.fr
A major Parisian gay venue where it may be difficult to get in. Disco Queen (Mon), Over Kitsch (Sun), and house and electro the rest of the week.

SHOPPING

Avenue Montaigne (E E3)
Synonymous with luxury and elegance, the avenue is lined with boutiques representing some of the world's best couturiers and designers.
Vuitton (no. 22)
→ Tel. 01 45 62 47 00
Christian Dior (no. 30)
→ Tel. 01 40 73 54 44
Nina Ricci (no. 39)
→ Tel. 01 40 88 67 60
Chanel (no. 42)

→ Tel. 01 47 23 74 12

Ladurée (E F3)
→ 16, rue Royale (8th)
Tel. 01 42 60 21 79
Mon-Thu 8.30am–7.30pm;
Fri-Sat 8am–8pm; Sun 10am–7pm; also 75, av. des Champs-Élysées (E D3) and 21, rue Bonaparte (A B2)
With Daloyau and Hermé, a contender for the title of 'world's best macarons'. They come in around 20 flavors (cognac, coffee, bitter chocolate, vanilla, rose petals, liquorice, etc.), served under kitsch Second Empire gildings.

Batignolles organic market (E F2)
→ Bd des Batignolles (between Rue Turin and Rue Puteaux)
Sat 7am–2pm
A market selling organic fruit, vegetables, cheese, and other healthy specialties such as wheatgrass juice. High prices, but good quality.

Les Caves Taillevent (E D2)
→ 199, rue du Faubourg-St-Honoré (8th)
Tel. 01 45 61 14 09
Mon-Sat 10am–7.30pm
A famous cellar with more than 1,500 labels from affordable wines from small vineyards to the rarest of grands crus. Also brandies and spirits.

LA DÉFENSE

ARC DE TRIOMPHE

MUSÉE CERNUSCHI

CITÉ DES FLEURS

e Grande Arche (Otto Spreckelsen, 1989), a empty cube like a emporary version of rc de Triomphe. Look or the huge concrete of the CNIT building), statues by Miró 'stabile' by Calder.

sée Jacquemart-é (E E2)

, bd Haussmann (8th) 45 62 11 59; Daily –6pm (9pm Mon, Sat) rivate collection of Jacquemart and rd André is housed magnificent nents of their Second e home. There are entury Dutch old

masters in the library, works of the 18th-century French School in the reception rooms, English paintings in the smoking room, while the Italian Renaissance is represented upstairs.

★ Musée Nissim-de-Camondo (E E2)

→ 63, rue de Monceau (8th) Tel. 01 53 89 06 50 Wed-Sun 10am–5.30pm The fabulous collection of Moïse de Camondo (1860–1935) is preserved in the banker's former house at the edge of the Parc Monceau. It is devoted to the decorative arts of the late 18th century and

includes furniture by Carlin and Riesener, ornate silverware, the celebrated Sèvres service known as the 'Buffon' and other priceless treasures.

★ Parc Monceau (E E2)

→ Daily 7am–10pm (9pm Sep; 8pm Oct-April) This gorgeous 18th-century park, remodeled in the 'English' style in the 19th century, is dotted with statues and antique ruins.

★ Musée Cernuschi (E E2)

→ 7, av. Vélasquez (8th) Tel. 01 53 96 21 50 Tue-Sun 10am–6pm From his extensive travels in Asia, the financier Henri Cernuschi (1821–96)

brought back about 5,000 works of art: ancient bronzes, funerary statuettes from the 10th and 11th centuries, etc. Don't miss the impressive 15-ft-high Amithaba Buddha (18th c.).

★ Cité des Fleurs (E F1)

→ 154, av. de Clichy or 59, rue La Jonquière (17th) Daily 7am–7pm (1pm Sun) Countryside and peace a couple of steps away from the noisy Avenue de Clichy. This 250-yard cobbled lane was lined with two-storey cottages in 1847 and each resident was asked to plant at least three flowering trees in his garden.

MUSÉE DU QUAI BRANLY

PALAIS DE TOKYO / MUSÉE D'ART MODERNE DE LA VILLE DE PARIS

★ Invalides (F F2)
→ Tel. 01 44 42 37 72; Wed-Mon 10am–5pm (6pm April-Sep, plus Tue 10am–9pm)
This golden dome (351 ft) can be seen for miles. Built under the order of Louis XIV in 1671–6, the Invalides served as a hospital for wounded soldiers. Today it contains the Dome and St-Louis churches, the tomb of Napoleon I, the Ordre de la Libération, Plans-Reliefs and Army museums, as well as the Charles-de-Gaulle history museum.

★ Musée Rodin (F F2)
→ 79, rue de Varenne (7th)
Tel. 01 44 18 61 10
Tue-Sun 9.30am–5.45pm

(4.45pm Oct-March)
One of the most charming museums in Paris, opened in Rodin's house, the 18th-century Hôtel Biron, two years after his death. Around 500 sculptures and 8,000 prints and drawings by the artist (1840–1917) are shown here by rotation. Some of his most important works, including Le Penseur (The Thinker) and Les Bourgeois de Calais (The Burghers of Calais) are on display in the garden, under the shade of the lime trees.

★ Tour Eiffel (F D1)
→ Mid-June to Aug: daily 9am–12.45am; Sep-mid-June: daily 9.30am–11.45pm

The symbol of the capital, erected in 1889 for the Universal Exhibition and still the tallest building in the city at 1,063 ft. From the top-floor observatory, you can see for 40 miles across Paris on a clear day. But it is from the base that you get a real sense of the magnitude of this gigantic steel structure. At the foot of the tower, the Champ-de-Mars, a park designed in 1908, stretches all the way to the École Militaire.

★ Trocadéro (F D1)
The impressive Palais de Chaillot (1937) dominates the Seine. Its two wings encircle the Trocadéro's

esplanade and house th[e] Musée de l'Homme (un[der] renovation until 2015), [the] Musée de la Marine an[d] since 2007, the Cité de l'Architecture et du Patrimoine. Beneath th[e] gardens, the aquarium, built for the 1878 Univer[sal] Exhibition, boasts 43 tanks, 10,000 fish and underground glass tun[nel]

★ Cité de l'Architectu[re] et du Patrimoine
→ Tel. 01 58 51 52 00; We[d-] Mon 11am–7pm (9pm Thu[)]
The Architecture and Heritage Museum hous[es a] spectacular collection [of] casts of ancient abbey doorways, huge bas-re[liefs]

F

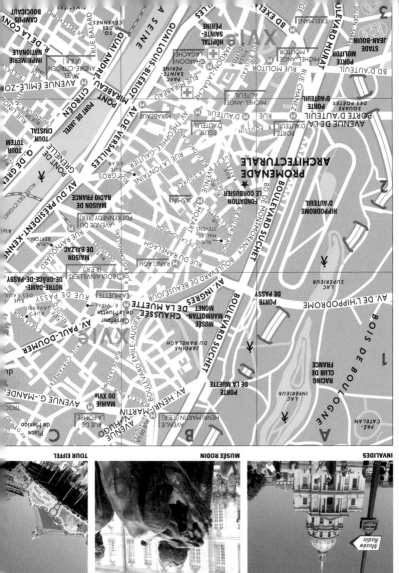

INVALIDES

Musée
Rodin

MUSÉE RODIN

TOUR EIFFEL

Map labels

CAMPUS BOUCICAUT
CAMPUS DE LA CONT...
IMPRIMERIE NATIONALE
P. DE LA CONT
RUE DES CÉVENNES
QUAI ANDRÉ-CITROËN
A SEINE
QUAI LOUIS-BLÉRIOT
QUAI DE LA
HÔPITAL SAINTE-PÉRINE
BD EXEL...
EXELMANS
JEAN-BOUIN
STADE JEAN-BOUIN
BOULEVARD MURAT
XVI
GEN...
DUGEN...

AVENUE ÉMILE-ZO...
RUE DE LINO...
RUE DES ENTREPRENEURS
JAVEL ANDRÉ-CITROËN
PONT MIRABEAU
RUE MIRABEAU
PARC SAINTE-PÉRINE
RUE SAINTE-PÉRINE
CHARDON-LAGACHE
CHARDON-LAGACHE
AV. VILL...
MICHEL-ANGE MOLITOR
PORTE MOLITOR
STADE MOLITOR
RUE MOLITOR
BD D'AUTEUIL
PORT DE JAVEL
TOUR CRISTAL
Q. DE GRE...
TOUR TOTEM
PONT DE GRENELLE
AV. DE VERSAILLES
PORT DE JAVEL
AGAR
RUE THÉOPHILE-GAUTIER
RUE LA FONTAINE
RUE GROS
AV. MIRABEAU
RUE
D'AUTEUIL
AUTEUIL
MICHEL-ANGE
PORTE D'AUTEUIL
SQUARE DES POÈTES
PORTE D'AUTEUIL
AVENUE DE LA D'AUTEUIL
ÉGLISE D'AUTEUIL
PORTE D'AUTEUIL
POUSSIN
RUE CHANEZ
ALLÉE DES CYGNES
MAISON DE RADIO FRANCE
AV. DU PRÉSIDENT-KEN...
AVENUE DU PDT KENNEDY (RER)
JASMIN
RUE MOZART
FONDATION LE CORBUSIER
PROMENADE ARCHITECTURALE
BD DE MONTMORENCY
HIPPODROME D'AUTEUIL
BOULEVARD SUCHET
BOULEVARD D'AUTEUIL
RUE GEORGES-SAND
RUE DE LA SOURCE
RUE RAYMOND
RUE BERTON
RUE DES VIGNES
RUE DE BOULAINVILLIERS
RUE MALLET STEVENS
RUE DU RANELAGH
BOULEVARD DE BEAUSÉJOUR
RANELAGH
MAISON DE BALZAC
NOTRE-DAME-DE-GRÂCE-DE-PASSY
RUE DE PASSY
LA MUETTE
BOULEVARD ÉMILE-AUGER
AV. INGRES
BOIS DE BOULOGNE
LAC SUPÉRIEUR
AV. DE L'HIPPODROME
RUE DES EAUX
RUE RAYNOUARD
RUE GAVARNI
RUE DE PASSY
AV. PAUL-DOUMER
CHAUSSÉE DE LA MUETTE
MUSÉE MARMOTTAN-MONET
Carrefour de la Muette
R. VITAL
BOULEVARD SUCHET
PORTE DE PASSY
PORTE DE LA MUETTE
JARDINS DU RANELAGH
RACING CLUB DE FRANCE
LAC INFÉRIEUR
PRÉ-CATELAN
RUE CORTAMBERT
AVENUE G.-MANDE
AVENUE VICTOR-HUGO
RUE DE LA POMPE
RUE DE LA TOUR
XVIe
MAIRIE DU XVIe
AVENUE HENRI-MARTIN (R.E.R.)
PORTE DE LA MUETTE
AV. HENRI-MARTIN
AVENUE HENRI-MARTIN
RUE DE LA POMPE
PLACE de Mexico
AV. D'EYLAU
TROC...
JARDINS DU RANELAGH

Ministries, embassies and other major institutions are the most important occupants of the 7th arrondissement. Here too is the great gilded dome of the Invalides, whose classical outline dominates the vast esplanade. To the east is the École Militaire and the Champ de Mars, whose edges are bordered with fine town houses overlooking the Eiffel Tower. On the opposite bank, the stylish 1930s complex of the Trocadéro brings the fantastic view to a close. Further out the opulent 16th arrondissement is very grand in the north around the Avenue Foch, but a bit more provincial in Passy and Auteuil.

LA CAVE DE L'OS À MOELLE

TOKYO EAT

RESTAURANTS

Au Pied de Fouet (F F2)
→ 45, rue de Babylone (7th)
Tel. 01 47 05 12 27; Mon-Sat noon–2.30pm, 7–11pm
A former coaching inn with creaking wood floors and checked tablecloths, serving mainly brown food: soup, lentil salad, steak with mashed potatoes, prunes poached in wine, etc. Entrées €8.90–11.90.

La Cave de l'Os à Moelle (F C3)
→ 181, rue de Lourmel (15th)
Tel. 01 45 57 28 28; Tue-Sun noon–3pm, 7.30–10.30pm
A restaurant-wine cellar with outstanding vintages on display and a selection of pâtés, ham, sausages, crudités and cheese as well as a dish of the day. Help yourselves and sit at one of the communal tables. Also picnic hampers to take out. Prix fixe €28.

Café Constant (F E1)
→ 139, rue St-Dominique (7th); Tel. 01 47 53 73 34
Daily 8am–10.30pm (kitchen noon–5pm, 7–11pm)
This is not just another neighborhood café and not just another chef. Michelin-starred Christian Constant opened this restaurant so we could

regale ourselves at modest prices. The long list of dishes is marked on huge boards. Go to the bar for a glass of wine while waiting for a table if you haven't reserved. Prix-fixe lunch €16, €23; entrées €16.

Noura (F E1)
→ 27, av. Marceau (16th)
Tel. 01 47 23 02 20
Daily 8am–midnight
One of the best Lebanese restaurants in Paris. Plates of meze, chicken chawarma with tabouleh and sweet pastries. 'Snack corner' if you're in a hurry, and the Noura deli across the road. Excellent wines, all available by the glass. Entrées €18–25.

Le Grand Pan (F E4)
→ 20, rue Rosenwald (15th)
Tel. 01 42 50 02 50; Mon-Fri noon–2pm, 7.30–11pm
This neo-bistro is popular with lovers of good food. The meat is of exceptional quality and the organic wines are drawn from small casks. Entrées €14 (lunch), €20–25.

Le Chalet des Iles (F A1)
→ Bois de Boulogne, lower lake (16th)
Tel. 01 42 88 04 69
Tue-Sat noon–2.30pm, 7.30–10.30pm; Sun noon–2.30pm (daily noon–

ÉRAL BEURET   **LAURENT DUBOIS**   **BLACK BLOCK**

2.30pm, 7.30–10.30pm in summer)
A chalet given to the Empress Eugénie by Napoleon, and perched on an island in the middle of the Bois de Boulogne. Magical setting and good classic cuisine. Prix-fixe €21–27 (weekday lunch); entrées €16–29.

L'Ami Jean (F E1)
→ 27, rue Malar (7th)
Tel. 01 47 05 86 89; Tue-Sat noon–2pm, 7pm–midnight
A small bistro with Basque memorabilia for decor and the talented Stephane Jégo in the kitchen, who produces an outstanding seasonal Basque cuisine. Entrées €35–42; prix fixe €42, €80.

TEAROOM, CAFÉS, BARS

Carette (F D1)
→ 4, pl. du Trocadéro-et-du-11-Novembre (16th)
Tel. 01 47 27 98 85
Daily 7.30am–11.30pm
A traditional tearoom founded in 1927, popular with the chic older ladies of the *seizième*, who come here in their finest attire for brunch and Carette's famous chocolate macaroon. Snacks too.

Club des Poètes (F F1)
→ 30, rue de Bourgogne

(7th); Tel 01 47 05 06 03
Mon-Fri noon–3pm, 8pm–last customer; Sat 8pm–last customer. Times vary
On Tuesdays, Fridays and Saturdays at exactly 9pm, this unpretentious little bar turns into a venue for poetry lovers, with some choice vintages to accompany the verse.

Tokyo Eat (F D1)
→ 13, av. du Président Wilson (16th)
Restaurant: Tue-Sun noon–3pm, 8–11.30pm (10.30pm Sun); cafeteria: noon–midnight (8pm in winter and outside exhibition dates)
The Palais de Tokyo hides a hi-tech, ultra-trendy cafeteria and restaurant, with low lacquered tables and long picture windows. Glorious terrace.

Général Beuret (F E3)
→ 9, pl. du Général-Beuret (15th); Tel. 01 42 50 28 62
Daily 8am–2am
A cheerful and colorful bar at the far end of the 15th, and a friendly place for a break at any time of day. The zinc bar is a museum piece and there is an outside terrace.

Le Bréguet (F F3)
→ 72, rue Falguière (15th)
Tel. 01 42 79 97 00; Mon-Sat 5pm (6.30pm Sat)–1.30am
A pleasant surprise in the rather boring 15th

arrondissement, this is a colorful bar, where a bunch of regulars (mostly students) meet for a pint or a cocktail.

Eiffel Tower Champagne Bar (F D1)
→ Top of the Eiffel Tower (7th); Daily noon–10pm
End your visit to the Eiffel Tower with a glass of champagne, 1,000 ft above ground.

MOVIE THEATER

La Pagode (F F2)
→ 57, rue de Babylone (7th)
Tel. 01 45 55 48 48
etoile-cinema.com
This extraordinary pagoda was built in 1896 by F.-E. Morin, owner of the Bon Marché department store, as a present to his wife. Today it is a movie theater with two rooms – the Japanese room is classified as a historical monument. Mainstream movies in the original language. Tea garden.

SHOPPING

Laurent Dubois (F D2)
→ 2, rue de Lourmel (15th)
Tue-Fri 9am–1pm (1.30pm Fri), 4-7.45pm; Sat 8.30am–7.45pm; Sun 9am–1pm
A cheesemonger whose

name is a byword in Paris: his fabulous store has around 300 varieties. They will vacuum-pack your purchases if you're about to travel.

Black Block (F D1)
→ 13, av. du Pdt Wilson (16th); Tel. 01 47 23 37 04
Tue-Sun noon–midnight
This concept store inside the Palais de Tokyo is meant to remind you of, in the owner's own words, 'a petrol station in the Stockholm suburbs'. Forget the unappealing tag, André's gift boutique is quite fun, selling design objects, books, toys, vintage clothing and records – you name it.

Franck et Fils (F C1)
→ 80, rue de Passy (16th)
Tel. 01 44 14 38 00; Mon-Sat 10am–7pm (8pm Sat)
Three floors of fashion, with the most exclusive brand names at street level (Dior, Chanel, etc) and trendy designer clothes upstairs (Isabelle Marant, Irie Wash, etc). There's also a café.

Book market (F E4)
→ 104, rue Brancion (15th)
Sat-Sun 9am–6pm
Beneath the horse market pavilion at the Vaugirard slaughterhouses are 60 stalls selling second-hand and rare books.

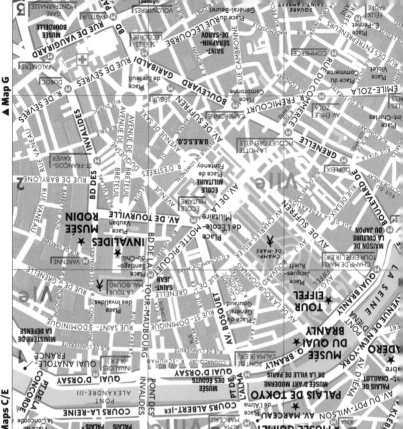

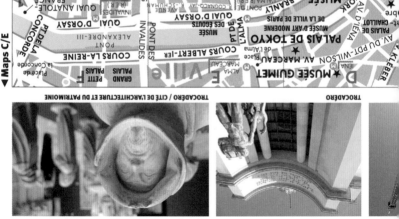

TROCADÉRO

TROCADÉRO / CITÉ DE L'ARCHITECTURE ET DU PATRIMOINE

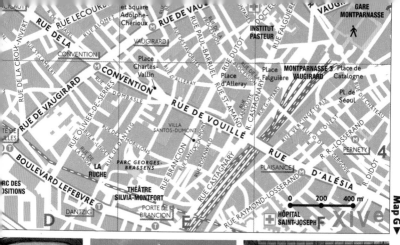

ÉE GUIMET

ARCHITECTURAL WALK

PARC ANDRÉ-CITROËN

from Roman times up
e 18th century. Upstairs
models of recent and
emporary buildings,
temporary exhibitions.
usée
Quai Branly (F D1)
→ *quai Branly (7th)*
1 56 61 70 00; Tue-Sun
—7pm (9pm Thu-Sat)
21st century's first
building project in
(2006) was conceived
an Nouvel. It resembles
nt footbridge over a
cre garden filled with
, following the curve of
eine. The museum's
hall, a 600-ft-long
space with partitions,
setting for the

valuable collections: 3,500
exhibits on the arts and
civilizations of Africa, Asia,
the Americas and Oceania.
★ Palais de Tokyo (F D1)
→ *13, av. du Président-Wilson*
(16th); Tel 01 53 67 40 00
Tue-Sun noon–midnight
Musée d'Art Moderne
11, av. du Président-Wilson
(16th); Tel 01 47 23 38 86;
Tue-Sun 10am–6pm
In the west wing of this
1937 building is the
experimental Palais de
Tokyo, a 'laboratory' of
contemporary creation. In
the east wing, the Museum
of Modern Art has an
extensive collection of
20th-century masters:

Matisse, Picasso, Braque,
Dufy, Delaunay, etc.
★ Musée Guimet (F D1)
→ *6, pl. d'Iéna (16th)*
Tel. 01 56 52 53 00
Wed-Mon 10am–5.45pm
Opened in 1889 thanks to
the generosity of Émile
Guimet (1836–1918) and
restored between 1996 and
2000, it displays antiquities
from India, Afghanistan
and Southeast Asia.
★ Architectural
walk (F B2)
The quiet southern part of
the 16th arrondissement
has some architectural
treasures from the late 19th
and early 20th centuries,
such as the Art Nouveau

designs by Hector Guimard
in the Rue la Fontaine (nos
14, 19 & 60); the geometric
shapes of Mallet-Stevens
in the street named after
him; and the pure forms of
Le Corbusier at the Villa La
Roche (*10, square du Dr-*
Blanche), which houses the
Le Corbusier Foundation.
★ Parc
André-Citroën (F C3)
→ *Balloon tel. 01 44 26 20 00*
Daily 9am–sunset
A 35-acre park on the bank
of the Seine, opened in
1992 on the site of the
former Citroën factory.
In good weather a balloon
offers great views from
500 ft up.

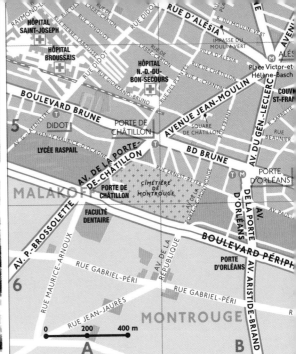

FONDATION HENRI-CARTIER-BRESSON

CIMETIÈRE DU MONTPARNASSE

★ **Musée Maillol (G** B1)
→ 59-61, rue de Grenelle (7th);
Tel. 01 42 22 59 58
Daily 10.30am–7pm (9pm Fri)
Two museums in one, with the sculptures, paintings, and early drawings of Aristide Maillol (1861–1944) along with the art collection belonging to his muse Dina Vierny. The latter includes works by Degas, Kandinsky, Matisse, Dufy and Foujita.

★ **Tour Montparnasse (G** B3)
→ Roof access via rue de l'Arrivée (15th); Daily 9.30am–11.30pm (10.30pm Oct-March)
At 689 ft, this is the highest tower block in France and a

rare example of a Parisian skyscraper, whose aesthetic value has been a source of debate ever since it was completed in 1973. Stunning panoramic views from the 59th floor roof terrace and the bar below.

★ **Musée Bourdelle (G** A2)
→ 16, rue Antoine-Bourdelle (15th); Tel. 01 49 54 73 73
Tue-Sun 10am–6pm
Antoine Bourdelle (1861–1929), a student of Rodin, lived here from 1885, where he completed Hercules the Archer, The Dying Centaur as well as busts of Beethoven. His living quarters, garden,

studio and a contemporary wing designed by Christian de Portzamparc (1992) contain over 500 bronzes, casts and works in marble.

★ **Fondation Cartier (G** C3)
→ 261, bd Raspail (14th)
Tel. 01 42 18 56 50; Tue-Sun 11am–8pm (10pm Tue)
This incredible construction of glass and steel, designed by Jean Nouvel in 1994, holds fascinating temporary exhibitions of contemporary art.

★ **Fondation Henri Cartier-Bresson (G** B3)
→ 2, impasse Lebouis (14th)
Tel. 01 56 80 27 00; Tue-Fri, Sun 1pm–6.30pm (8.30pm

Wed); Sat 11am–6. 45pm
The foundation set up by the great photographer (1908–2004) is located in a beautiful, early 20th-century artist's studio, where exhibitions of documentary photography are held. Occasional drawing and sculpture exhibitions too.

★ **Cimetière du Montparnasse (G** B3)
→ 3, bd Edgar-Quinet (14th);
Daily 8am (8.30am Sat, 9am Sun)–6pm (daily 8am–5.30pm in Nov-mid-March)
A tribute to the writers and artists who contributed to this area's renown in the 19th and 20th centuries

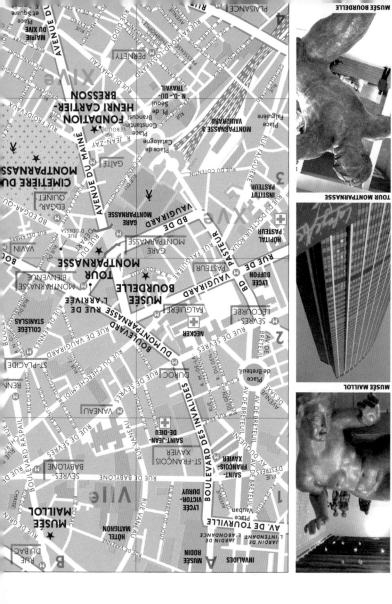

MUSÉE BOURDELLE

TOUR MONTPARNASSE

MUSÉE MAILLOL

Map Labels

VIIe

MUSÉE MAILLOL
RUE DU BAC
RUE DE VARENNE
BOULEVARD RASPAIL
RUE DE SÈVRES
BOULEVARD DES INVALIDES

MUSÉE RODIN
INVALIDES
JARDIN DE L'INTENDANT
JARDIN DE L'ABONDANCE

HÔTEL MATIGNON
RUE VANEAU
LYCÉE VICTOR-DURUY
Place Vauban
AV. DE TOURVILLE

SEVRÈS-BABYLONE
ST-FRANÇOIS-XAVIER
SAINT-FRANÇOIS-XAVIER

RUE DE BABYLONE
BOULEVARD DES INVALIDES
AV. DE BRETEUIL
AV. DE SAXE
AVENUE DE BRETEUIL

VANEAU
DUROC
SAINT-JEAN-DE-DIEU
RUE DE SÈVRES

ST-PLACIDE
COLLÈGE STANISLAS
RUE DE VAUGIRARD
BOULEVARD DU MONTPARNASSE
RUE DE L'ARRIVÉE

NECKER
FALGUIÈRE
SÈVRES-LECOURBE
Place de Breteuil

MUSÉE BOURDELLE
TOUR MONTPARNASSE
MONTPARNASSE BIENVENUE
GARE MONTPARNASSE
BD DE VAUGIRARD
RUE DE VAUGIRARD
BD PASTEUR
RUE FALGUIÈRE

LYCÉE BUFFON
HÔPITAL PASTEUR
INSTITUT PASTEUR
RUE DU DOCTEUR ROUX
RUE DU COTENTIN

VAVIN
BOUL
RUE D'ODESSA
RUE DU DÉPART
GARE MONTPARNASSE
GAÎTÉ

EDGAR-QUINET
BD EDGAR-QUINET
CIMETIÈRE DU MONTPARNASSE
AVENUE DU MAINE

FONDATION HENRI CARTIER-BRESSON
Place de Catalogne
Place LEBOUIS
Imp. Constantin Brancusi
Pl. de Séoul
N.-D.-DU-TRAVAIL
MONTPARNASSE 3 VAUGIRARD
Place Fálguière

RUE DU CHÂTEAU
PERNETY
GEORGES BRAQUE
PLAISANCE
RUE DE VOUILLÉ

XIVe
XVe
MAIRIE DU XIVe
Place du XIVe
AVENUE DU MAINE

RUE VERCINGÉTORIX
RUE R. LOSSERAND
RUE DE L'OUEST

RUE DE LA GAÎTÉ
RUE DU MAINE
RUE JEAN-ZAY

1 2 3 4

A B

From the aristocratic Faubourg St-Germain, the boutique-lined Rue du Cherche-Midi and Rue du Bac lead down to Montparnasse and its tower. Around the Vavin intersection are several cozy cafés and Art Nouveau brasseries, a legacy from the Belle Époque when this was the bohemian and artistic nerve center of the city. Beyond the Montparnasse Cemetery are the Place Denfert-Rochereau, with its replica of Bartholdi's famous Lion of Belfort, and the busy pedestrian Rue Daguerre. To the south, the 14th arrondissement extends down to the attractive Parc Montsouris, and is studded with gastronomic bistros.

ENZO

LA COUPOLE

RESTAURANTS

Ti Jos (G B3)
→ 30, rue Delambre (14th) Mon-Sat 11.30am–2.30pm, 7–11.30pm (closed Tue pm); Sun 7–11pm; pub: Mon, Wed-Sat 7pm–2am
One of the best Breton crêperies in the area, opened in 1937. Rustic oak furniture throughout the dining room, buckwheat savory pancakes, cider and Breizh cola, and Celtic music in the basement pub. Entrées €4–15.

Enzo (G B4)
→ 72, rue Daguerre (14th) Tel. 01 43 21 66 66 Mon 7.30–10.30pm; Tue-Fri noon–2.30pm, 7–10.30pm; Sat noon–2.30pm
Enzo's trattoria only has room for a few tables and high chairs so reserving is a good idea. The pasta dishes are good but the pizzas are sensational (and can be taken out). Excellent value for money. Entrées €8–13.

La Cabane à Huîtres (G B2)
→ 4, rue Antoine-Bourdelle (15th); Tel. 01 45 49 47 27 Tue-Sat noon–2.30pm, 7–10.30pm
A tiny eating house of the type usually found in the southwest of France

rather than beside the Montparnasse tower. It belongs to Francis Dubourg, oyster farmer and restaurateur. Try his traditionally cultivated oysters (or foie gras, or smoked duck breast) with a glass of Entre-deux-mers. Prix fixe €19.50.

La Cantine du Troquet (G A4)
→ 101, rue de l'Ouest (14th) Tel 01 45 40 04 98 Mon-Sat 11.45am–2.15pm, 7–10.45pm
No reservations are taken, so meet early at this boho-chic cafeteria, designed by Christan Etchebest. On the chalkboard: shrimps a la plancha, grilled pig's ears, rice pudding and other retro bistro dishes. Entrées €13–17.

La Cerisaie (G B3)
→ 70, bd Edgar-Quinet (14th); Tel. 01 43 20 98 98; Mon-Fri noon–2pm, 7–10pm
With only one room and a dozen tables close to one another this isn't the place for a romantic date. It is the right spot, however, if you want excellent regional classics from southwest France – milk-fed lamb from the Pyrenees with stuffed pimientos, goose breast with peaches, etc.

ERNAIRE

RUE D'ALÉSIA

P. BOURSAULT

Reserve. Entrées €16.

La Régalade (G B5)
→ 49, av. Jean-Moulin (14th)
Tel. 01 45 45 68 58
Mon 7–11pm; Tue-Fri
noon–2.30pm, 7–11pm
Fifteen years ago Yves
Camdeborde started
Paris's bistro revolution
with this small restaurant
dedicated to authentic
cooking. He has now left,
but Bruno Doucet retains
the exceptional quality of
the seasonal cuisine. The
place is still a favorite
with Parisian gourmets so
reservation is essential.
Prix fixe €34.

CAFÉS, BARS

Café Tournesol (G B3)
→ 9, rue de la Gaîté (14th)
Daily 8am–2am
A friendly café surrounded
by the theaters and sex
shops of the Rue de la
Gaîté, with outdoor
seating and a vibrant,
youthful atmosphere.

La Coupole (G B3)
→ 102, bd du Montparnasse
(14th); Daily 8am–midnight
(1am Thu-Sat)
A Parisian landmark.
The bohemian spirit of
the 1930s has long gone,
but the brasserie still
cuts a fine figure with its
33 pillars and Art Deco
furniture. Average cooking

so just go for a drink.

**La Closerie
des Lilas (G** C3)
→ 171, bd du Montparnasse
(6th); Tel. 01 40 51 34 50
Brasserie: daily noon–1am;
Café: 11am–1.30am
Gide, Hemingway, Lenin,
Beckett... each has a little
gold plaque celebrating
his presence in this
legendary brasserie
(dating to 1847), furnished
in dark wood. Piano bar
and a terrace screened off
by a dense hedge.

MOVIE THEATERS

Lucernaire (G C2)
→ 53, rue Notre-Dame-des-
Champs (6th)
Tel. 01 45 44 57 34; Mon-Fri
10am–10pm (12.30am Tue-
Fri); Sat 11am–12.30am;
Sun 3–10pm
A dynamic arts venue at
the heart of the student
quarter that surrounds
the Rue Vavin. It is home
to live theater, photo
exhibitions, art-house
and experimental movies.
There's also an
inexpensive restaurant
and a quirky bar with a
terrace on the street.

L'Entrepôt (G A4)
→ 7-9, rue F.-de-Pressensé
(14th); Tel. 01 45 40 07 50
lentrepot.fr
This is a fantastic space

with a movie theater
(independent films,
lectures and debates),
a good restaurant with a
shady garden, and a bar
with a varied program of
live events – jazz, rock,
improvised theater, etc.

SHOPPING

**Rue du
Cherche-Midi (G** B1)
A long street whose
north end has some
well-known shoe stores:
Fausto Santini (no. 4 ter),
Robert Clergerie (no. 5),
Accessoire Diffusion
(no. 6), David Orcel
(no. 7) and others.
Karine Dupont sells her
high-fashion handbags
at no. 16.

P. Boursault (G B5)
→ 71, av. du Général-Leclerc
(14th); Tel. 01 43 27 93 30;
Tue-Fri 9am–1pm, 3.30-
7.30pm; Sat-Sun 9am–
7.30pm (1pm Sun)
Over 150 varieties of
cheese, many of them
goat's, and also the hard-
to-find Termignon blue.
Camemberts with
Calvados, and Époisses
ripen slowly downstairs
in the cellars. Vacuum-
packing service available.

Rue d'Alésia (G B4)
A commercial street in

the south of the 14th
arrondissement with cut-
price stores. Some stock a
variety of brands, but there
are also Sonia Rykiel (no.
112), Chevignon (no. 122)
and Georges Rech (no.
100).

**Boucherie Hugo
Desnoyer (G** B4)
→ 45, rue Boulard (14th)
Tel. 01 45 40 76 67
Tue-Sat 7am–1pm, 4–8pm
One of the best butchers
in Paris and the supplier
of some of the city's best
restaurants: milk-fed veal,
Salers beef, pork roast,
etc. But also everything
you need for a picnic, from
wine to dry sausages.

Le Bon Marché (G B1)
→ 24, rue de Sèvres (7th)
The chic, medium-size
department store has a
terrific deli, **La Grande
Épicerie de Paris**
(Mon-Sat 8.30am–9pm)
selling top-of-the-range
produce from all over the
world, as well as snacks
to eat in or take out.

Mamie Gâteaux (G B2)
→ 66, rue du Cherche-Midi
(6th); Tel. 01 45 44 36 63
Tue-Sat 11.30am–6pm
An unusual combination
of antique shop and
tearoom, it sells
collectibles – old cookie
tins, ancient recipe books
– and homemade cakes.

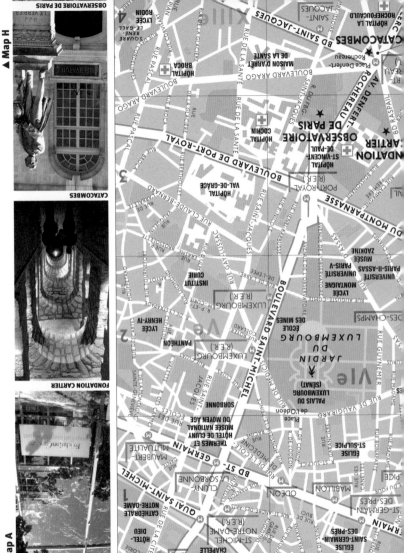

▲ Map H

OBSERVATOIRE DE PARIS

CATACOMBES

FONDATION CARTIER

▼ Map A

Map (labels)

Map H
- OBSERVATOIRE DE PARIS
- LE VERRIER
- U.J.

Map D / main map area:

- BD SAINT-JACQUES
- SAINT-JACQUES
- ROCHEFOUCAULD
- CATACOMBES
- ROCHEREAU
- Place Denfert-Rochereau
- AV. DENFERT-ROCHEREAU
- BD RASPAIL
- LYCÉE RODIN
- SQUARE RENÉ-LE-GALL
- RUE DU PLAN
- RUE DE LA GLACIÈRE
- RUE DE LA SANTÉ
- BOULEVARD ARAGO
- MAISON D'ARRÊT DE LA SANTÉ
- HÔPITAL BROCA
- RUE PASCAL
- RUE LEBRUN
- BOULEVARD ARAGO
- RUE DU FBG-SAINT-JACQUES
- OBSERVATOIRE DE PARIS
- HÔPITAL COCHIN
- QUARTIER
- FONDATION
- HÔPITAL ST-VINCENT-DE-PAUL
- RUE DE LA SANTÉ
- RUE CLAUDE-BERNARD
- BOULEVARD DE PORT-ROYAL
- RUE SAINT-JACQUES
- RUE DE LA GLACIÈRE
- RUE BROUSSAIS
- RUE DU MONTPARNASSE
- PORT-ROYAL (R.E.R.)
- HÔPITAL VAL-DE-GRÂCE
- INSTITUT CURIE
- RUE GAY-LUSSAC
- AVENUE DE L'OBSERVATOIRE
- MUSÉE ZADKINE
- UNIVERSITÉ PARIS-II-ASSAS
- UNIVERSITÉ PARIS-V
- LYCÉE MONTAIGNE
- LUXEMBOURG (R.E.R.)
- BD ST-MICHEL
- BOULEVARD SAINT-MICHEL
- ÉCOLE DES MINES
- PANTHÉON
- LYCÉE HENRY-IV
- Ve
- VIe
- JARDIN DU LUXEMBOURG
- PALAIS DU LUXEMBOURG (SÉNAT)
- SORBONNE
- RUE SOUFFLOT
- RUE DES ÉCOLES
- MUSÉE NATIONAL DU MOYEN ÂGE
- HÔTEL DE CLUNY
- THERMES ET
- CLUNY-LA SORBONNE
- MAUBERT-MUTUALITÉ
- BD ST-GERMAIN
- RUE DE MÉDICIS
- Place de l'Odéon
- ODÉON
- RUE DE CONDÉ
- RUE DE VAUGIRARD
- ÉGLISE ST-SULPICE
- RUE BONAPARTE
- MABILLON
- ST-GERMAIN-DES-PRÉS
- ÉGLISE SAINT-GERMAIN-DES-PRÉS
- SAINT-MICHEL
- QUAI SAINT-MICHEL
- CATHÉDRALE NOTRE-DAME
- QUAI DE LA CORSE
- HÔTEL-DIEU
- SAINTE-CHAPELLE
- CITÉ
- ST-MICHEL NOTRE-DAME (R.E.R.)
- ROCHEREAU

PARC MONTSOURIS

**CITÉ INTERNATIONALE
UNIVERSITAIRE**

...delaire, Maupassant, ...voir and Sartre (buried ...ther), Beckett, Duras, ...ine and Gainsbourg ...mong those resting in ...9-acre cemetery, ...ed in 1824.

...atacombes (G C4)
→ *av. du Colonel-Henri-Rol-*
...uy (14th); Tel. 01 43 22 47
...e-Sun 10am–5pm
..., for this is the land of ...ead', reads the sign ...e the entrance to this ...ossuary, created from ...work of underground ...ies between 1786 and ...when the parish ...teries were closed for ...ns of hygiene. A dark ...nth of passages is

lined with the skulls and femurs of some 6 million Parisians, stacked up in the 19th century.

★ Observatoire de Paris (G C3)
→ *77, av. Denfert-Rochereau*
(14th); Tel. 01 40 51 22 21
Visits by appt one Sat per
month
Founded by the statesman Colbert in 1667 on a site that was then outside the city, the national observatory continues to function today. The austere building was designed by Claude Perrault in the classical style fashionable in the reign of Louis XIV. When it is open to the

public, it offers a unique opportunity to explore the night sky over Paris in the company of astronomers.

★ Parc Montsouris (G C5)
→ *Mon-Fri 8am–sunset*
Sat-Sun 9am–sunset
One of the city's largest parks (37 acres) laid out by Alphand as part of Haussmann's redesigning of Paris, which planned a large open space at each of its four cardinal points. It is designed to resemble an English garden, complete with miniature lake, band-stand and other attractions.

★ Cité Internationale Universitaire (G C6)
→ *17, bd Jourdan (14th)*

Tel. 01 44 16 64 00
Daily 7am–10pm
This huge campus opened in 1925 and accommodates some 5,600 students of around 130 different nationalities. The 40 so-called 'houses' are arranged in an 80-acre park: some of them reflect the vernacular architecture of the countries they represent while others are important contemporary works such as those of Switzerland (1930) and Brazil (1954), both designed by Le Corbusier. The impressive Maison Internationale (1936) houses a theater, a café and an attractive terrace.

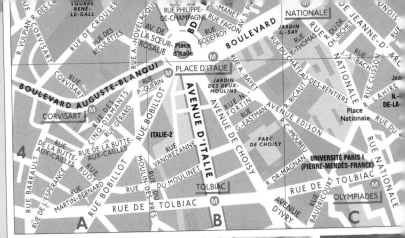

MANUFACTURE DES GOBELINS

CITÉ DE LA MODE ET DU DESIGN

BIBLIOTHÈQUE NATIONALE

★ Institut du Monde Arabe (H B1)

→ 1, rue Fossés-St-Bernard (5th); Tel. 01 40 51 38 38 Tue-Sun 10am-6pm

This amazing building, designed by Jean Nouvel and Architecture Studio (1987), is an adaptation of an Arab-Hispanic concept using contemporary materials. Its museum of Arabian-Islamic civilization and art, library and bookstore explore the culture of the Arab countries. The strikingly modern Mobile Art Pavilion, on the forecourt, was designed by Zaha Hadid as exhibition space. Events also include movies, dance and concerts.

★ Arènes de Lutèce (H A1)

→ 49, rue Monge (5th) Daily 9am-9.30pm (8am-5.30pm Oct-April)

Discovered in 1869 while clearing the Rue Monge, these remains of a Gallo-Roman amphitheater (1st c.) were included in a public garden in 1896.

★ Jardin des Plantes (H B1)

→ Rue Cuvier, rue Buffon and place Valhubert (5th) Open from sunrise to sunset

In 1640, the royal garden of medicinal plants became the first park in Paris to open its gates to the public. It has been home to the Muséum National d'Histoire Naturelle since 1793. Facing the Grande Galerie (1889), the flower beds stretch over a third of a mile, leading to the two large glasshouses (Mexican and Australian), designed by Charles Rohaut de Fleury in 1834. There is also a wonderful maze to get lost in, and a zoo.

★ Muséum National d' Histoire Naturelle (H B2)

→ 36, rue Geoffroy-St-Hilaire (5th); Tel. 01 40 79 30 00 Wed-Mon 10am-6pm (5pm Galerie d'Anatomie)

Inside the vast Evolution Gallery, the collection of stuffed animals is astonishingly realistic. the east side, the Galle Comparative Anatomy Paleontology remains as it was in the 19th ce with old-fashioned dis cases and handwritte labels for the exhibits latter comprise a fascin survey of vertebrate li and a brilliant tour thr the world of fossils an dinosaurs. Also of not the Children's Gallerie and the Mineralogica Geological galleries.

★ Grande Mosquée de Paris (H B2)

→ 1, pl. du Puits-de-l'Er (5th); Tel. 01 43 31 18 14 Sat-Thu 9am–noon, 3–6

H

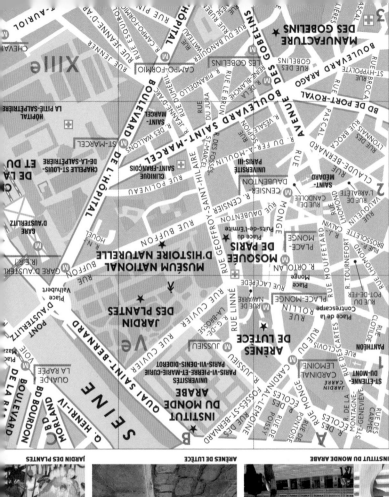

JARDIN DES PLANTES

ARÈNES DE LUTÈCE

INSTITUT DU MONDE ARABE

Map text

XIIIe

Ve

MANUFACTURE DES GOBELINS ★

MOSQUÉE DE PARIS ★

MUSÉUM NATIONAL D'HISTOIRE NATURELLE ★

JARDIN DES PLANTES ★

ARÈNES DE LUTÈCE ★

INSTITUT DU MONDE ARABE ★

BOULEVARD SAINT-MARCEL

BOULEVARD ARAGO

BOULEVARD DE L'HÔPITAL

AVENUE DES GOBELINS

BD DE PORT-ROYAL

QUAI SAINT-BERNARD

BOULEVARD DE LA RÂPÉE

QUAI DE LA RÂPÉE

SEINE

BD BOURDON

BD HENRI-IV

BD MORLAND

PONT D'AUSTERLITZ

GARE D'AUSTERLITZ

LA PITIÉ-SALPÊTRIÈRE (HÔPITAL)

HÔPITAL DE-LA-SALPÊTRIÈRE

CHAPELLE ST-LOUIS-DE-LA-SALPÊTRIÈRE

CLINIQUE SAINT-FRANÇOIS

UNIVERSITÉ PARIS-III

UNIVERSITÉ PARIS-VI-PIERRE-ET-MARIE-CURIE

UNIVERSITÉS PARIS-VII-DENIS-DIDEROT

PANTHÉON

Place Valhubert

Place du Puits-de-l'Ermite

PLACE MONGE

PLACE-MONGE

Place de la Contrescarpe

Place Monge

RUE MONGE

RUE MOUFFETARD

RUE GEOFFROY-SAINT-HILAIRE

RUE CUVIER

RUE LINNÉ

RUE BUFFON

RUE POLIVEAU

RUE CENSIER

RUE DAUBENTON

RUE JUSSIEU

CARDINAL LEMOINE

ST-ÉTIENNE-DU-MONT

JUSSIEU

CENSIER-DAUBENTON

CAMPO-FORMIO

SAINT-MARCEL

ST-MARCEL

CHEVALERET

RUE JENNER

RUE JEANNE-D'ARC

RUE DU BANQUIER

RUE PASCAL

RUE CLAUDE-BERNARD

RUE BROCA

RUE LHOMOND

RUE ORTOLAN

RUE LACÉPÈDE

RUE DE NAVARRE

R.G.-DE-LA-BROSSE

RUE DESCARTES

RUE CLOVIS

RUE CLOTILDE

RUE DES ÉCOLES

RUE DE PONTOISE

RUE DE POISSY

RUE DE LA MONTAGNE-STE-GENEVIÈVE

RUE STE-GENEVIÈVE

RUE DES CARMES

RUE DES FOSSÉS-ST-BERNARD

FOSSÉS-ST-MARCEL

R. DU FER-À-MOULIN

RUE POT-DE-FER

R. TOURNEFORT

RUE L'ARBALÈTE

RUE VAUQUELIN

RUE ROLLIN

RUE LACÉPÈDE

RUE DU JURA

VOIE MAZAS

R. AURIOL

The busy streets of the Mouffetard district lie beyond the Jardin des Plantes and the Grande Mosquée. From there the broad Avenue des Gobelins leads to the Place d'Italie, the heart of the 13th arrondissement. Nearby is the former village of the Butte-aux-Cailles, and out toward the Porte de Choisy is the Parisian Chinatown (1970). The eastern edge is bordered by the Seine and the old industrial wastelands of Bercy and Austerlitz, which are now home to the huge BNF (Bibliothèque Nationale de France) – opened in 1997 – and, more recently, the Cité de la Mode et du Design and a new university campus.

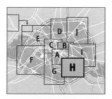

LAO LANE XANG

LE TEMPS DES CERISES

RESTAURANTS

Lao Lane Xang (H C4)
→ 105, av. d'Ivry (13th)
Tel. 01 45 85 19 23; Tue-Sun noon–3pm, 7–10.30pm
This Laotian restaurant in the Asian 13th arr. is a real find, serving delicately cooked dishes redolent of the scents and spices of the Mekong Valley. There is another, smarter, slightly more expensive version of it opposite. Entrées €5–12; prix fixe €10–12.50 (lunch).

Chez Gladines (H A4)
→ 30, rue des Cinq-Diamants (13th); Tel. 01 45 80 70 10; Sun-Tue noon–3pm (4pm Sun), 7pm–midnight; Wed-Sat noon–3pm (4pm Sat), 7pm–1am
An informal Basque restaurant that gets so busy you may have to share a table. Huge salads and tasty specialties from the southwest. Excellent value for money. Entrées €6.50–13.

Le Temps des Cerises (H A4)
→ 18-20, rue de la Butte-aux-Cailles (13th)
Tel. 01 45 89 69 48; Mon-Fri 11.45am–2.30pm, 7.15–11.45pm; Sat 7.15–11.45pm
A workers' cooperative opened in 1976, welcoming and relaxed, and still a bit libertarian. Hearty home cooking: Normandy-style black pudding, braised pork cheek. Prix fixe €10–15 (lunch), €15–23; entrées €10–18.

Les Délices d'Aphrodite (H A2)
→ 4, rue de Candolle (5th)
Tel. 01 43 31 40 39
Daily noon–2.30pm, 7–11pm
The gourmet taverna of the Mavrommátis brothers, masters of Hellenic gastronomy, with fantastic moussaka and superb platters of meze. Entrées €17–25.50; prix fixe €17.50–19.50 (lunch).

L'Avant-Goût (H B4)
→ 26, rue Bobillot (13th)
Tel. 01 53 80 24 00; Tue-Sat 12.15–2pm, 7.45–10.45pm
Chef-owner Christophe Beaufront's cuisine is a delight: inventive, flavorful and with a Japanese accent after a recent visit there – try his signature dish: pork pot-au-feu with spices. Perfect wine list (Beaufront's wine shop and deli is across the road, at no. 37). Reserve. Entrées €19; prix fixe €14.50 (lunch), €32.

L'Ourcine (H A3)
→ 92, rue Broca (13th)
Tel. 01 47 07 13 65; Tue-Sat noon–2pm, 7.30–10.30pm

TEAROOM OF THE GRANDE MOSQUÉE

BATOFAR

TANG FRÈRES

Sylvain Daniere learned his trade under the formidable Yves Camdeborde at La Régalade, and now runs his own restaurant with obvious passion, inspired by seasonal produce and working directly with small wine producers. Exceptional cuisine. Reservation advised. Prix fixe €26 (lunch), €34.

TEAROOMS, BARS, CLUBS

Tearoom of the Grande Mosquée (H B2)
→ 39, rue Geoffroy-St-Hilaire (5th)
Tel. 01 43 31 38 20
Daily 9am–midnight
Small tables in the courtyards under the olive trees, Moorish interior and sofas inside the mosque. Come here for a tagine, crunchy honey-soaked baklavas or simply for a mint tea.

La Salle à Manger (H A2)
→ 138, rue Mouffetard (5th)
Tel 01 55 43 91 99; Mon-Fri 8.30am–4.30pm (7pm July-Sep); Sat-Sun 8.30am–7pm
A good-value bakery-cum-brasserie with large tables to share at breakfast, teatime or brunch on weekends. Pretty terrace

on the square, at the heart of the Mouffetard market.

La Folie en Tête (H A4)
→ 33, rue de la Butte-aux-Cailles (13th); Daily 5pm–2am (midnight Sun)
A laid-back café in the old village of Butte-aux-Cailles, a healthy distance from a Paris that is both inflated in price and overly trendy. Imaginatively decorated with wooden musical instruments from all over the world.

Merle Moqueur (H A4)
→ 11, rue de la Butte-aux-Cailles (13th)
Daily 5pm–2am
An institution on the Butte, this noisy, buzzing, friendly bar is always packed. Music from the 1970s–90s and a long list of rum cocktails.

Batofar (H E3)
→ Opposite 11, quai F.-Mauriac (13th)
Tel. 01 53 60 17 30
Totally avant-garde when it opened in 1999, Batofar is still the best known of the trendy floating clubs anchored at the foot of the BNF. Steel hull and interior, with eclectic mix of electronic, jazz, world or rock music. On deck, La Cantine bar with DJs. Deckchairs and tables on the quayside in summer.

SHOPPING

Paris Jazz Corner (H B1)
→ 5, rue de Navarre (5th)
Tel. 01 43 36 78 92
Tue-Sat noon–8pm
An authority on jazz music since 1991, with more than 40,000 CDs and LPs covering the entire history of jazz and its subgenres. Also blues and gospel.

Les Abeilles (H A4)
→ 21, rue de la Butte-aux-Cailles (13th); Tel. 01 45 81 43 48; Tue-Sat 11am–7pm
The small shop of a Parisian beekeeper, whose bees work in the 13th arrondissement and the Bois de Vincennes. Also honey from Mexico, Tasmania, Australia, etc.

Tang Frères (H C4)
→ 44 and 48, av. d'Ivry (13th)
Tel 01 45 70 80 00
Mon-Sat 10am–8.30pm
The most famous Asian supermarket, with an amazing range of products. One floor up is the Olympiades, a mini shopping center with clothes and gadgets. Another shop at no. 48.

Bercy Village (H F3)
→ Cour St-Émilion (12th)
Stores: daily 11am–9pm
A truly pleasant destination, the Cour St-Emilion is a row of 42 listed stone

warehouses in the style of a small village. Most of these former Bercy chais (wine cellars) have been turned into shops or restaurants.

ART GALLERIES

Rue Louise-Weiss (H D3)
→ Galleries: Tue-Sat 11am–7pm; louise13.fr
This street and the adjacent ones (Chevaleret and Duchefdelaville) contain a dozen contemporary design and art galleries. Joint private views every two months.

Les Frigos (H E3)
→ 19, rue des Frigos (13th)
les-frigos.com
The former refrigerated warehouses ('frigos') of Bercy and their thousands of free square feet of space have been turned into working areas for 200 artists. A gallery and a café are open from time to time, and the artists open their studios to the public each May.

Les Voûtes
→ lesvoutes.org
In four vaulted cellars of the Frigos, at the bottom of a pretty garden, is an arts venue for cultural events of all kinds.

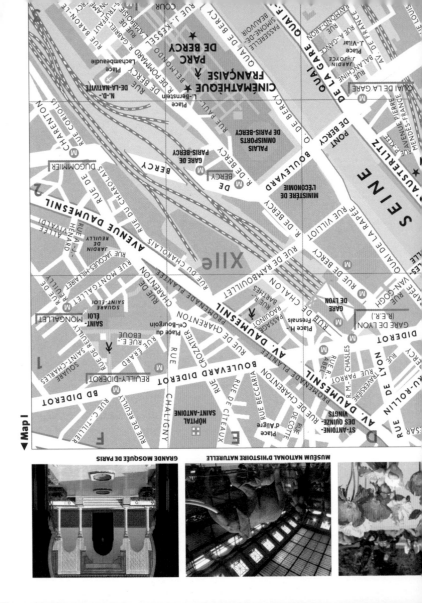

▲ Map I

GRANDE MOSQUÉE DE PARIS

MUSÉUM NATIONAL D'HISTOIRE NATURELLE

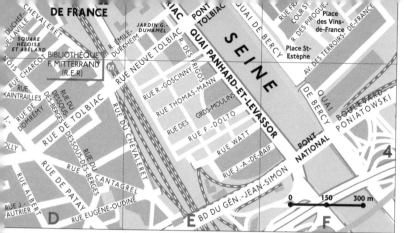

Map labels visible: DE FRANCE, JARDIN G. DUHAMEL, PONT TOLBIAC, QUAI DE BERCY, RUE DES PIROGUE., COUR ST.-ÉMILION, Place des Vins-de-France, Place St-Estèphe, SEINE, QUAI PANHARD-ET-LEVASSOR, DE BERCY, QUAI DE BERCY, BOULEVARD PONIATOWSKI, SQUARE HÉLOÏSE ET ABÉLARD, BIBLIOTHÈQUE F. MITTERRAND (R.E.R), M., RUE ÉMILE-DURKHEIM, RUE R.-GOSCINNY, RUE THOMAS-MANN, GRDS-MOULINS, RUE DES, RUE F.-DOLTO, RUE WATT, RUE J.-A.-DE-BAIF, PONT NATIONAL, RUE NEUVE TOLBIAC, RUE DES FRIGOS, RUE DU CHEVALERET, RUE DE TOLBIAC, RUE DU CHEVALERET, RUE DE BERCY, RUE DE PATAY, RUE DE CANTAGREL, RUE ALBERT, RUE J.-FAUTRIER, RUE EUGÈNE-OUDINE, BD DU GÉN.-JEAN-SIMON, D, E, F, 4

0 — 150 — 300 m

PARC DE BERCY

CINÉMATHÈQUE FRANÇAISE

s temple to the Muslim gion was the first to be t in Paris (1922–6) and rranged around a rtyard and indoor dens. It has a rich diterranean influence: saics, the finest lattice k and cedarwood ings – a rich interior ated by local craftsmen. room and hammam e previous page).

Manufacture Gobelins (**H** A3)
→ 2, av. des Gobelins (13th)
01 44 08 53 49; Tue-Sun 0am–4.30pm; tour of the kshops: Tue-Thu 1.15pm, om and 3pm
royal tapestry

workshop, founded by Henry IV, is still operating. You can visit the workshops and the gallery, with temporary exhibitions of antique and contemporary tapestries and furniture.

★ **Cité de la Mode et du Design** (**H** D2)
→ 28-36, quai d'Austerlitz (13th)
The old warehouses known as the Magasins Généraux (1907) have been converted into an exhibition and conference area for fashion and design. Housed in a metallic and glass shell designed by Jakob and MacFarlane, this is one of the few buildings in Paris

right on the river.

★ **Bibliothèque Nationale de France** (**H** D3)
→ Quai François-Mauriac (13th); Tel. 01 53 79 59 59
Tue-Sat 10am–8pm;
Sun 1–7pm; Visitors' center in the Hall Est
The four 'book towers' were devised by Dominique Perrault and have been holding some ten million works (more than 260 miles of shelving) since 1995. The reading rooms are arranged around a surprising indoor garden. Temporary exhibitions.

★ **Parc de Bercy** (**H** E3)
→ Quai de Bercy (12th)

Mon-Fri 8am–sunset;
Sat-Sun 9am–sunset
In 1994 the Bercy wine storehouses gave way to the development of a 33-acre park, which includes botanical gardens, an orchard, a kitchen garden and a Romantic-style garden.

★ **Cinémathèque Française** (**H** E3)
→ 51, rue de Bercy (12th)
Tel. 01 71 19 33 33; Shows Mon, Wed-Sat noon–7pm (10pm Thu); Sun 10am–8pm
A must for cinephiles in an amazing building by Frank Owen Gehry (1994).
Movies, exhibitions, retrospectives, etc.

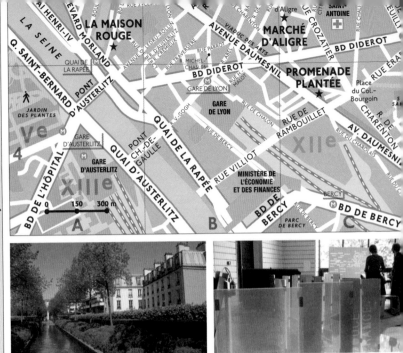

PROMENADE PLANTÉE

CITÉ NATIONALE DE L'HISTOIRE DE L'IMMIGRATION

★ **Place
de la Bastille** (❶ B3)
The storming of the 14th-
century fortress in 1789
caused the square on
which it stood to become
the symbol of the French
Revolution. At its center,
the July column (164 ft),
topped by the *Génie de la
Liberté*, stands in homage
to the victims of the *Trois
Glorieuses* (the revolution
of July 27, 28 and 29, 1830).
★ **Opéra Bastille** (❶ B3)
➔ 120, rue de Lyon (12th)
Tel. 01 40 01 19 70
Performances: 08 92 89 90 90
operadeparis.fr
The work of architect Carlos
Ott, Paris's second opera

house, commissioned by
Mitterrand to make opera a
more popular and
accessible form of
entertainment, opened on
the symbolic date of July
13, 1989. The round white
vessel is most magnificent
at night when lights shine
through its glass windows.
★ **La Maison Rouge** (❶ A3)
➔ 10, bd de la Bastille (12th)
Tel 01 40 01 08 81; Wed-Sun
11am-7pm (9pm Thu)
Contemporary art
exhibitions in 13,000 sq. ft
of a former factory built
around a central residential
building – the 'red house'.
Pleasant tearoom, The
Rose Bakery.

★ **Port de l'Arsenal** (❶ A3)
Built in the early 19th
century around the former
moat of the Bastille prison,
and marking the southern
end of the Canal St-Martin,
the dock was where all the
wood was landed for the
furniture workshops of the
Faubourg St-Antoine. Since
1983 it has been a marina
handling about 900 boats
a year. A terraced garden
runs along its east bank.
★ **Faubourg
St-Antoine** (❶ C3)
➔ Rue du Faubourg-St-
Antoine (11th/12th); Often
closed pm and weekends
From 1471, this *faubourg*
(lit. 'fake town') gathered

around its abbey a grow
community of craftwork
allowed to work outside
the constraints of any
corporation. Gilders,
carpenters and varnishe
still remain here. Look o
for the Cour du Bel-Air at
56; Passage du Chantier
no. 66; and the pretty C
de l'Étoile-d'Or at no. 75
★ **Le Lieu du Design** (❶ C
➔ No. 74; Tel. 01 40 41 51
Mon-Sat 1–6pm (7pm Sat)
Exhibitions and conferer
celebrate all aspects of
design. This space is at
Cour des Bourguignons
whose iron and glass
construction is a relic of
19th-c. industrialization

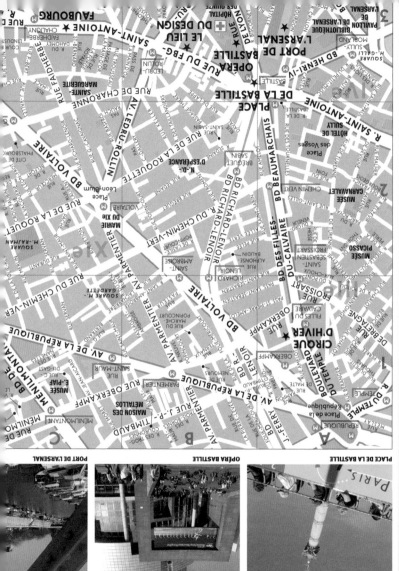

PLACE DE LA BASTILLE

OPÉRA BASTILLE

PORT DE L'ARSENAL

Place de la Bastille is where the capital's dedicated nightlife begins, and restaurants and cafés line the streets around the square. Further east take a peek at the maze of courtyards and passageways along the Rue du Faubourg-St-Antoine. Cabinet-makers, for whom this area is renowned, still work here, now alongside designers, architects, graphic designers and stylists. To the north is one of the most famous and most visited cemeteries in the world, the 109-acre Père-Lachaise. Back west, the Oberkampf area has become one of the hippest places to hang out in Paris, night or day.

BISTROT PAUL-BERT

CHATEAUBRIAND

RESTAURANTS

Little Paris-Hanoi (I D2)
→ 9, rue de Mont-Louis (11th); Tel. 01 46 59 01 40 Mon-Sat noon–2.30pm, 7–10.30pm
The younger brother of the celebrated Vietnamese diner Paris Hanoi (74, rue de Charonne, I C3) is a more spacious space near the Père-Lachaise Cemetery. Wonderfully fresh food and terrific bò bún. Entrées €9–11.

Amici Miei (I B2)
→ 44, rue St-Sabin (11th) Tel. 01 42 71 82 62; Tue-Sat noon–2.30pm, 7.30–11pm
A quiet street, yet seemingly a converging path for all of Paris to meet in this busy, noisy spot for its pizza bianca (no tomato) and fresh pasta. Both the food and the wine list reflect the restaurant's Sardinian roots. Entrées €9–17.

Bistrot Paul-Bert (I C3)
→ 18, rue Paul-Bert (11th) Tel. 01 43 72 24 01; Tue-Sat noon–2pm, 7.30–11pm
A typical Parisian bistro with old posters on the walls and a busy kitchen. Try the pork cutlet with wholegrain mustard and the now famous Paris-Brest for dessert. Prix fixe €18 (lunch), €36.

Jacques Mélac (I C2)
→ 42, rue Léon-Frot (11th) Tel. 01 43 70 59 27; Tue-Sat noon–3.30pm, 8–11.45pm
Vines cover the façade of Chez Mélac, where you can find saucisse sèche from the Aveyron region, cheese from Cantal and good house specials are served with a glass of wine. Prix fixe €15; entrées €13–18.

Mansouria (I C3)
→ 11, rue Faidherbe (11th) Tel. 01 43 71 00 16 Mon-Tue 7.30–11pm; Tue-Sat noon–2pm, 7.30–11pm
This renowned Moroccan restaurant, run by Fatéma Hal, serves exceptional couscous and tajines. Entrées €15–19; prix fixe €28, €36.

Mama Shelter (I E2)
→ 109, rue de Bagnolet (20th); Tel. 01 43 48 45 45 Daily noon–midnight (11pm Sun)
The latest hype liner, moored in the 20th arrondissement, has a decor by Philippe Starck that evokes a New York loft and simple dishes (confit of duck, fish and chips, club sandwich) conceived by master chef Alain Senderens. Also two bars, pizzas (noon–1.30am), and brunch on Sunday. Entrées €14–29.

CHARBON

RUE KELLER / GAËLLE BARRÉ

BAGUE DE KENZA

Chateaubriand (I B1)
→ 129, av. Parmentier (11th)
Tel. 01 43 57 45 95; Tue-Sat, two sittings (by reservation): 7.30pm, 9.30pm
One of the hottest neo-bistro tables in town, this soberly decorated spot belongs to Basque chef Inaki Aizpitarte, the rising star of modern cuisine. His daily-changing menu is very original, with combinations of unlikely flavors – foie gras in miso soup, teriyaki salmon with berries and beetroot. At no. 131 is Aizpitarte's tapas bar, Le Dauphin. Prix fixe €55.

CAFÉS, BARS, CONCERTS

Le Baron rouge (I B3)
→ 1, rue Theophile-Roussel (12th); Tel 01 43 43 14 32 Tue-Fri 10am-2pm, 5-10pm; Sat-Sun 10am-10pm (4pm Sun)
A wine bar frequented by all the locals when the Aligre market is in full swing, with wines from the cask, oysters (Sat-Sun Oct-Easter), cheeses and charcuterie too. You'll be lucky to find a seat.

Pure Café (I C3)
→ 14, rue Jean-Macé (11th) Tel 01 43 71 47 22; Mon-Sat 7am (8am Sat)-2am; Sun

10am-midnight
Away from the action is this horseshoe-shaped zinc bar with an inviting, luminous dining room.

Le Lèche-Vin (I B2)
→ 13, rue Daval (11th)
Tel. 01 43 55 06 70
Tue-Sat 6.30pm-2am
Religious decorations of all sorts cover this bar. Loud music and cheap draught beer.

Le Balajo (I B2)
→ 9, rue de Lappe (11th)
Tel. 01 47 00 07 87
Mon 2-7pm; Tue, Thu 7.30-2am (4.30am Thu); Wed 8pm-2am; Fri-Sat 11pm-5.30am; balajo.fr
Opened in 1936, the 'Bal à Jo' revives the tradition of the Sunday afternoon dance, with live accordion music. Evening classes: salsa (Tue, Thu), rock'n' roll (Wed). Clubbing Fri-Sat; tea dance Mon.

Pop in (I A2)
→ 105, rue Amelot (11th)
Tel. 01 48 05 56 11
Daily 6.30pm-1.30am
A choice of evenings in this relaxed and youthful bar with lounge upstairs and concert hall in the cellar (small groups pop-rock-funk Mon-Thu; DJs Fri-Sat; open mike Sun).

Café Charbon (I B1)
→ 109, rue Oberkampf (11th)

Tel. 01 43 57 55 13; Daily 9am-2am (4am Wed-Sat)
One of the trailblazing cafés when Oberkampf first became trendy, set in a fin-de-siècle room with industrial decor, gas lighting and a zinc bar.

SHOPPING

Isabel Marant (I B3)
→ 16, rue de Charonne (11th)
Tel. 01 49 29 71 55; Mon-Sat 10.30am-7.30pm; also at 1, rue Jacob (A B2) and 47, rue de Saintonge (B E2)
This French fashion artist combines elegance with originality. Her modern, feminine designs are influenced by various ethnic styles.

Rue Keller (I B2)
The street with broad appeal: young manga fans, fashionistas and gothic tribes.

Gaëlle Barré
→ 17, rue Keller (11th)
Tel. 01 43 14 63 02
Tue-Sat 11.30am-7.30pm
In her workshop-boutique, Gaëlle offers retro fashion that is both romantic and feminine. Uses gorgeous prints, with a beautiful finish. Children's clothes as well.

Merci (I A2)
→ 111, bd Beaumarchais (11th); Tel. 01 42 77 00 33

Mon-Sat 10am-7pm
At the back of a courtyard, a chic, ethical concept-store selling clothes, second-hand or designer furniture, limited editions. All the profits go to charity. Go to Old Book Café for a break and cakes.

Lulu Berlu (I A1)
→ 2, rue du Grand-Prieuré (11th); Tel. 01 43 55 12 52 Mon-Sat 11am-7.30pm
A treasure trove of toys for nostalgic adults. From Star Wars heroes and rows of Japanese robots, all the magic is here, from the 1950s to the present.

Bague de Kenza (I B1)
→ 106, rue St-Maur (11th);
Tel. 01 43 14 93 15
Daily 9am (2pm Fri)-9pm; also 173, rue du Faubourg-St-Antoine (I C3)
The best Algerian tearoom-patisserie in Paris has a wide choice of delicate, flavored cakes and savory specialties that are incredibly hard to resist. Tearoom next door.

Cooperativa Cisternino (I B1)
→ 108, rue St-Maur (11th)
Mon-Sat 10am-1.30pm, 4.30-8pm
If you have had enough of French cuisine, indulge in Italian cheese and quality charcuterie at very reasonable prices.

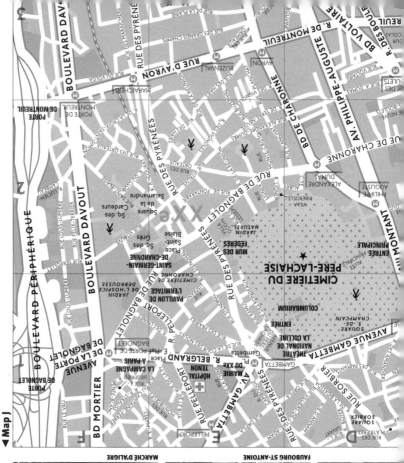

MARCHÉ D'ALIGRE

FAUBOURG ST-ANTOINE

VOLAILLE
BOUCHERIE
TRIPERIE CHARCUTERIE

CITÉ L'IMMIGRATION / AQUARIUM

CIMETIÈRE DU PÈRE-LACHAISE

CIRQUE D'HIVER

...ubourg.

...arché d'Aligre (I C3)
...e and Pl. d'Aligre (12th)
...un 7am–1.30pm
...ly market offering the
...t prices in the capital.
...mall Place d'Aligre
...s to life early morning
...lorists and sellers of
...-brac. On the Rue
...re you'll need to fight
...way through the
...s to get to the fruit
...egetable stalls. The
...Beauvau (1777), where
...tchers and cheese
...s are, is more relaxed.
**...menade
...ée** (I B3–F4)
...y 8am (9am Sat-Sun)–

An elevated, almost 3-mile-
long walkway from the start
of the Avenue Daumesnil
to the city's edge, on a
railway line that closed in
1969. The path goes over
viaducts and footbridges,
past planted beds and wild
undergrowth. Past the
Jardin de Reuilly, it
descends to street level
and enters a tunnel before
joining a cycle trail leading
to the Bois de Vincennes.
**★ Cité Nationale de
l'Histoire de
l'Immigration** (I F4)
→ 293, av. Daumesnil (12th)
Tel. 01 53 59 58 60; Tue-Sun
10am–5.30pm (7pm Sat-Sun)
Housed in a palatial

building at the Porte Dorée,
this museum lays out the
story of French immigration
since the 19th century
using photos and films for
an interactive experience.
Tropical aquarium in the
basement.
**★ Cimetière
du Père-Lachaise** (I D2)
→ Bd de Ménilmontant (20th)
Mid-March-Oct: daily 8am
(8.30am Sat, 9am Sun)–6pm;
Nov-mid-March: daily 8am–
5.30pm
With its shaded avenues,
undergrowth and winding
paths, this famous Parisian
cemetery (1804) is like a
miniature world. The most
extravagant of tombs stand

alongside more modest
burial sites. Molière,
Balzac, Chopin, Proust,
Éluard, Edith Piaf and Jim
Morrison are among those
resting in this fascinating
garden of the dead.
★ Cirque d'Hiver (I A1)
→ 110, rue Amelot (11th)
Tel. 01 47 00 28 81
This stunning circus
was built by Hittorff,
opened by Napoleon III
in 1852, acquired by the
Bouglione brothers in 1934
and has now been partially
returned to its initial
purpose. Two original
statues remain: Bosio and
Duret's Le Guerrier and
Pradier's L'Amazone.

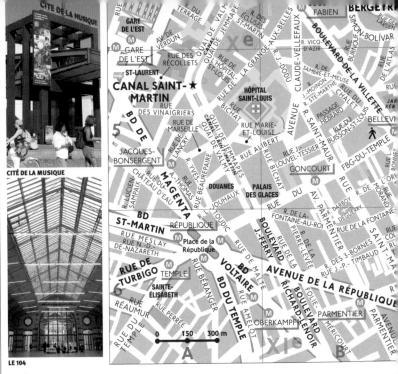

CITÉ DE LA MUSIQUE

LE 104

★ **Canal St-Martin** (J A5)
Carved out between 1822
and 1825, at the request of
Napoleon I to provide the
people of Paris with drinking
water, this canal has
become one of the capital's
most romantic spots. Its
planted banks and series of
locks, the metal foot bridges
and little gardens spread
over 3 miles are reminiscent
of a Paris that has now
disappeared. Perfect for a
walk on Sundays when the
banks are pedestrianized.

★ **Parc de la Villette** (J D2)
→ 221, av. Jean-Jaurès (19th)
One of the most amazing
landscaped gardens in
Paris, completed in 1991,

on the site of the former
slaughterhouses of La
Villette. A decidedly urban
park, it was designed as a
'garden city', whose lawns
come to life each summer
with concerts and a free
open-air film festival. The
blue path of the 'cinema
promenade' snakes its way
over 2 miles, crossing ten
themed gardens. A
pleasant cycle track follows
the Canal de l'Ourcq for 15
miles, all the way to Meaux.

★ **Cité des Sciences
et de l'Industrie** (J C2)
→ 30, av. Corentin-Cariou
(19th); Tel. 01 40 05 80 00
Tue-Sun 10am–6pm (7pm Sun)
Since 1986, this huge

museum has revealed the
secrets of science to
children and grown-ups,
with interactivity as its
keyword. The exhibition
'Explora' introduces several
themes (space, the ocean,
etc.). In 'Cité des Enfants',
participatory exhibits and
games (reserve) encourage
children to get to grips with
scientific information. Plus
workshops, a planetarium
and film projections on the
hemispheric 4,000-sq.-ft
screen of the Géode.

★ **Cité de la
Musique** (J D2)
→ 221, av. Jean-Jaurès (19th)
Tel. 01 44 84 44 84; Tue-Sun
noon (10am Sun)–6pm

A site dedicated to mus
in all its forms. Opened
1997, the museum offe
musical stroll from the
Renaissance to the end
the 19th century. Equip
with headphones, you
to hear the various
instruments displayed
glass cabinets in front
you. Also a concert hal
with a worldwide progr

★ **Le 104** (J B2)
→ 104, rue d'Aubervillier
(19th); Tel. 01 53 35 50 0
The impressive buildin
(1873), once a funeral
parlor, is now an imme
arts center and perform
space of over 250,000
ft. Its aim is to make th

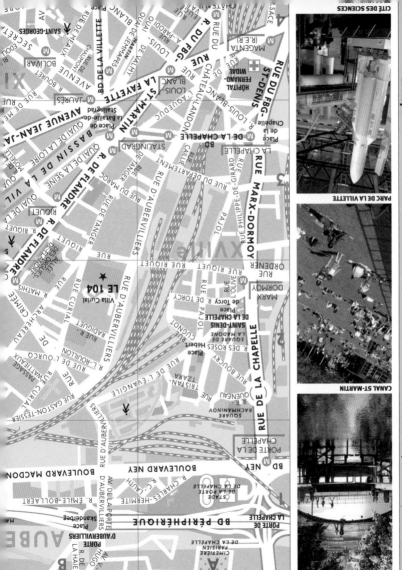

CITÉ DES SCIENCES

PARC DE LA VILLETTE

CANAL ST-MARTIN

Canal St-Martin / Belleville / Ménilmontant

Along the canals, Paris past and Paris present stand side by side. The Canal St-Martin is full of old-fashioned charm yet hip boutiques and cafés abound on its banks. The Canal de l'Ourcq continues as far as La Villette, a thoroughly 20th-century 'garden city' that's suddenly appeared out of nowhere. Further south the Parc des Buttes-Chaumont, renovated in 1864 to rehabilitate the surrounding slum area, has given birth to a respectable residential district. Below it are the old working-class villages of Belleville and Ménilmontant, with new Asian and Middle-Eastern influences and a busy market on Boulevard de Belleville.

LA BOULANGERIE

CHEZ PRUNE

RESTAURANTS

Lao Siam (J C5)
→ 49, rue de Belleville (19th); Tel. 01 40 40 09 68 Daily noon–3pm, 7–11.30pm
People in the know all agree that Lao Siam serves some of the best Thai food in Paris, delicately scented with spices, basil, ginger, coconut and lemongrass. Entrées €7–11.

New Nioullaville (J B5)
→ 32, rue de l'Orillon (11th) Tel. 01 40 21 98 38; Daily noon–3pm, 7pm–12.30am
A Belleville institution, this huge place is renowned for its trolleys of steaming dishes in the evening. Endless menu. Entrées €7–18.

Le Verre Volé (J A5)
→ 67, rue de Lancry (10th) Tel. 01 48 03 17 34; Daily 10.30am–2am (kitchen noon–2.30, 7–11pm)
This pioneer of bistro-wine bars is still going strong. The wine list is excellent and the tiny kitchen delivers pretty good French cuisine too. The place is small and very popular, so reserve. Entrées €13–24.

Maria Luisa (J A5)
→ 2, rue Marie-et-Louise (10th); Tel. 01 44 84 04 01

Mon–Thu noon–2.30pm, 8–11pm; Fri–Sun noon–2.30pm, 7.30–11.30pm (10.30pm Sun)
With a light dining room and attractive terrace, this restaurant by the canal serves delicious thin-crusted pizzas. Entrées €11–15.

Mon Oncle le Vigneron (J C5)
→ 71, rue Rébeval (19th) Tel. 01 42 00 43 30; Daily 11am–2.30pm, 8–9.30pm
A restaurant-deli run by a friendly Franco-Japanese couple, selling good wines from small vineyards, regional produce and a freshly made dish of the day. Reserve for dinner. Entrées €9–13 (lunch), prix fixe €30 (dinner).

La Boulangerie (J C6)
→ 15, rue des Panoyaux (20th); Tel. 01 43 58 45 45 Tue–Fri noon–2pm, 8–10.30pm; Sat 8–10.30pm
In a former rustic bakery, this restaurant offers delicate and inventive dishes. Daily-changing menu for lunch; monthly for dinner. Prix fixe €15–18 (lunch), €35 (dinner).

Chez Vincent Cozzoli (J C4)
→ Parc des Buttes Chaumont (entrance opposite 43 av. S.-Bolívar), pavillon Puebla (19th); Tel. 01 42 02 22 45

R OURCQ   ANTOINE ET LILI   PÂTISSERIE DE L'ÉGLISE DEMONCY

Mon-Sat 8pm–last customer
Generous antipasti and mouthwatering carpaccios are the specialties of this unassuming Italian spot, in the heart of Buttes-Chaumont park. Idyllic terrace. Prix fixe €35–50.

CAFÉS, BARS

Chez Prune (J A5)
→ 36, rue Beaurepaire (10th) Tel. 01 42 41 30 47
Daily 8am (10am Sun)–2am
A place for the bohemian bourgeoisie to meet, with vintage decor. Dishes of the day for lunch and cold food only at night. Just as pleasant is Jemmapes, the other side of the canal.

La Sardine (J B5)
→ 32, rue Sainte-Marthe (11th); Tel 01 42 49 19 46;
Oct-June: Tue-Sun 9am (10am Sat-Sun)–2am; July-Sep: daily 9am (10am Sat-Sun)–2am
Relax on the terrace in what looks like the square of a small country town, with a beer and a platter of charcuterie, far from the bustle of the city.

Lou Pascalou (J C6)
→ 14, rue des Panoyaux (20th); Tel. 01 46 36 78 10
Daily 10am (11am Sat-Sun)–2am
Lou Pascalou opened in 1983, in an area where

nothing much was happening. Today this popular, no-nonsense yet cozy place has become a centerpiece of the quartier's life. Pleasant terrace. Live bands on Sundays.

Bar Ourcq (J B3)
→ 68, quai de la Loire (19th) Tel. 01 42 40 12 26; April-mid-Nov: Wed-Sun 3pm-midnight (2am Fri-Sat; 10pm Sun); mid-Nov-March: Sat 3pm–2am; Sun 3–10pm
When it's sunny, the 'patron' brings out the boules and the deck chairs along the banks of the Ourcq canal. DJ at weekends.

Rosa Bonheur (J B3)
→ Parc des Buttes-Chaumont (entry on Rue Botzaris) (19th) Tel. 01 42 03 28 67
Wed-Sun noon–midnight
A rarity in Paris, a modern-day guinguette in a park. Have a drink on the terrace before the DJ turns up the music in what's becoming the place to be seen in the 19th arrondissement.

CLUBS, CONCERTS

La Maroquinerie (J D6)
→ 23, rue Boyer (20th) Tel. 01 40 33 35 05
lamaroquinerie.fr
Up on the heights of

Ménilmontant is a high-voltage venue with events of all kinds: concerts, exhibitions and clubbing, complete with restaurant, bar and a pretty courtyard terrace. Nearby is another nightspot: La Bellevilloise, with two superb cafés.

Point Éphémère (J B4)
→ 200, quai de Valmy (10th) Tel. 01 40 34 02 48
pointephemere.org
An underground concert venue in a former cement works, with exhibitions and a bar-restaurant along the quayside, where the audience chat and stroll, drink in hand.

HAMMAM

Hammam Medina Center (J C3)
→ 43-45, rue Petit (19th) Tel. 01 42 02 31 05
Mon-Fri 11am–10pm; Sun 9am–7pm (women); Sat 10am–9pm (mixed)
Massage and oriental body-care by expert hands. A glass of hot mint tea will round off your pampering session nicely.

SHOPPING

Fashion along the Canal St-Martin (J A5)
Fashionistas in search of bohemian bourgeois

treasures will not miss out on Rue Beaurepaire (Liza Korn at no.19, Cotélac at no. 30) and Rue de Marseille (Maje at no. 6). The shops are also open on Sunday afternoons.

Antoine et Lili (J A5)
→ 95, quai de Valmy (10th) Tel. 01 40 37 41 55; Daily 11am–8pm (7pm Mon-Sun)
Facing the canal are the yellow, green and pink façades of three Antoine and Lili boutiques (art, children and fashion). It will be hard to resist the gorgeous colored prints and retro or ethnic styles.

Épicerie Le Caire (J C5)
→ 63, rue de Belleville (19th) Tel. 01 42 06 06 01
Tue-Sun 10am–10pm
Adel Moussa's grocery shop resembles a souk: olives, spices, semolinas, oriental specialties (borek with cheese, baklavas) and other delicacies.

Pâtisserie de l'Église Demoncy (J D5)
→ 10, rue du Jourdain (20th) Tel. 01 46 36 66 08
Mon-Fri 9am (8am Mon)–2pm, 3-7.45pm; Sat-Sun 9am-7.45pm (6.30pm Sun)
This pâtisserie opened in 1887, and generations of locals have been raving about its éclairs and tartlets ever since.

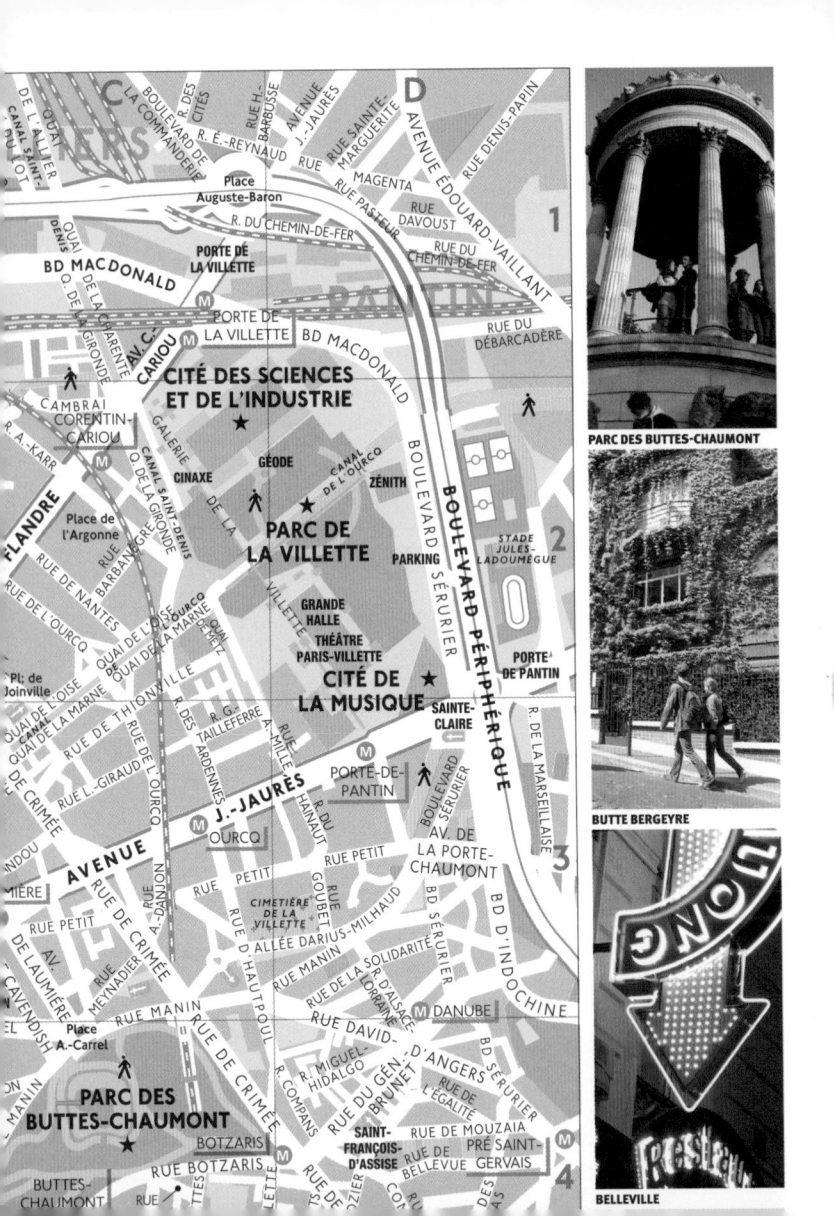

PARC DES BUTTES-CHAUMONT

BUTTE BERGEYRE

BELLEVILLE

Best of the best

What you have to experience in Paris

Push the door of a café

They are the center of social life and, for many patrons, a home away from home. Small neighborhood cafés are second to none for people (and soul) watching. You'll be spoilt for choice as they are extremely common – there is one café in Paris for every 200 inhabitants. As spring arrives, have a drink outside *en terrasse* and linger – only in a very touristy area will a surly waiter make it clear that unless you order again you should go.

→ *Café de la Mairie* (**A** B3); *Le Sancerre* (**D** B4)

Have dinner in a brasserie

Enter a world seemingly stuck in time, with its own strict hierarchy, from the old retainer opening oyster shells by the door to the squad of waiters in black pants and vests, white shirts and aprons. Relish the traditional classics of French cuisine – Alsatian sauerkraut, bouillabaisse, steak tartare – amid a fabulous decor of Art Deco brass, leather banquettes and mirrors.

→ *Le Terminus Nord* (**D** D4), opposite the Gare du Nord

Take a trip on a bateau-mouche

This is most enjoyable at night, when the crowds have evaporated and the city can be seen from a different perspective, with lights glowing under the bridges and projections from the boat onto the shoreline that make the buildings come alive.

→ *Look out for the gargoyles on the Pont-Neuf* (**A** C1) *and the statue (1856) of a Zouave (infantryman) from the Crimean War on the Pont de l'Alma* (**F** E1). *See also the Transportation section*

Eat an ice cream at Berthillon (**A** F3)

A welcome treat at all times of day, the cornets sold by the city's most famous ice-cream parlor never fail to delight, and they taste even better sitting on the quays of the Île St-Louis. Sorbets and ice cream come in some 75 imaginative flavors: marron glacé, fig, bitter chocolate, Earl Grey tea, gingerbread, pistachio, lemon and coriander, wild strawberry.

→ *Go in the morning in summer, to avoid the long queues*

Cycle with Vélib'

This self-service bicycle rental service has been a huge success since it began operating in 2005. For just €1.70, you can see the city from a different angle, enjoying its side streets, deserted

RIDING THE VÉLIB'

SECOND-HAND BOOK STALLS

LE BARON ROUGE

WAGG

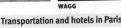

AIRPORTS

→ Tel. 39 50
aeroportsdeparis.fr
All practical information
for both Roissy and Orly
airports.
**Roissy-Charles-
de-Gaulle** (CDG)
Three terminals: 1, 2
(regular flights), and 3
(charter flights).
Orly (ORY)
Two terminals: Sud and
Ouest.
**Paris-Beauvais-Tillé
(BVA)**
→ Tel. 08 92 68 20 64
Shuttles to Porte Maillot
(**E** B2); €15; 75–90 mins;
aeroportbeauvais.com
Used by low-cost
airlines.

ACCESS TO AIRPORTS

*Unless otherwise stated, the
prices given are for a
standard double room en
suite, without breakfast. It is
recommended to reserve at
least a month in advance*

UNDER €75

Hostel Oops! (**H** A3)
→ 50, av. des Gobelins (13th)
Tel. 01 47 07 47 00
oops-paris.com
A bright and clean youth
hostel with colorful double
rooms and large dorms, all
en suite. Double rooms
€70–80, dorm €23–30/
pers, incl. breakfast.
**St-Christopher's
Inn** (**J** C3)
→ 159, rue de Crimée (19th)
Tel. 01 40 34 34 40
st-christophers.co.uk
This new English-owned
backpackers' hostel has
opened beside La Villette
in one of the former
warehouses known as the
Magasins Généraux. Six-

to ten-bed dormitories and
double rooms, some of the
latter en suite. Restaurant,
bar and internet café.
Double €70–110; dorms
€26–41/pers.
Hipotel Belleville (**J** B4)
→ 21, rue Vicq-d'Azir (10th)
Tel. 01 42 08 06 70; *hipotel.fr*
Not far from the Canal St-
Martin, this 45-year-old
hotel has 72 small rooms,
most with a view over a
verdant courtyard.
Breakfast is served in the
café next door. €36–56.
Hôtel Ste-Marie (**D** D6)
→ 6, rue de la Ville-Neuve
(2nd); Tel. 01 42 33 21 61
hotelsaintemarie.com
A small hotel near the
Grands Boulevards, with
20 basic but clean rooms.
From €62 (€46 with
shared bathrooms).
**Hôtel Bonséjour
Montmartre** (**D** B3)
→ 11, rue Burq
Tel 01 42 54 22 53
hotel-bonsejour-montmartre.fr

A friendly hotel right in the
center of Montmartre
with 34 rooms, four of
them with a balcony
overlooking the church of
Sacré-Coeur. €78 (€68
without bath).
Hôtel du Nord (**J** A5)
→ 47, rue Albert-Thomas
(10th); Tel. 01 42 01 66 00
hoteldunord-leparivelo.com
A hotel full of charm near
the Canal St-Martin, with
23 clean, cheerful rooms
and a very friendly staff.
Ten bicycles at the guests'
disposal. €69–82.
Hôtel Eldorado (**E** F1)
→ 18, rue des Dames (17th)
Tel. 01 45 22 35 21
eldoradohotel.fr
A friendly and attractive
hotel laid out around a
leafy courtyard. The decor
derives from items picked
up by the owners on their
travels. They also run the
excellent Bistro des Dames
downstairs at street level.
€73–82.

€75–140

Hôtel de Nesle (**A** C2)
→ 7, rue de Nesle (6th)
Tel. 01 43 54 62 41
hoteldenesleparis.com
A quirky hotel in a prime
location where the owner
has decorated each of the
20 rooms with frescoes to
illustrate such themes as
Molière, Africa, the Orient.
Rooms overlook either the
peaceful street outside or a
wonderful rustic garden to
the rear. €75–100.
Hôtel Esméralda (**A** D2)
→ 4, rue St-Julien-le-Pauvre
(5th); Tel. 01 43 54 19 20
This 17th-century town
house in a cobbled street
leads onto the pretty
Vivienne square and
houses an exquisite
19-room hotel. It has no
elevator, exposed stone
walls, red velvet sofas,
numerous plants, uneven
floors and ten rooms with
views of Notre-Dame.

From Roissy-CDG to the city center
RER B: €9.25
Roissybus: *Rue Scribe, by Opera métro station* (**C** D1); €9.10
Air France coach: *Porte Maillot* (**E** B2), *Étoile* (**E** C3), *Montparnasse* (**G** B3) €16.50
Taxi: *around € 50*

From Orly to the city center
Orlyval: *Orlyval then RER B; €10.90*
Orlybus: *In front of RER Denfert-Rochereau* (**G** C4); € 6.40
Air France coach: *Métro Invalides* (**F** F2), *Montparnasse* (**G** B3) €11.50
Taxi: *around €25*

BATEAU-MOUCHE PASSING THE LOUVRE

TRAMWAY ALONG THE PARC MONTSOURIS

The nine other smaller ones open out onto the courtyard. €75–105.

Les Marronniers (A B4)
→ *78, rue d'Assas (6th)*
Tel. 01 43 26 37 71
pension-marronniers.com
A family guest house in Paris is quite a rarity, and this one overlooks the Luxembourg gardens. It offers seven rooms, with breakfast and dinner included in the price. €78–83.

Familia Hôtel (A D3)
→ *11, rue des Écoles (5th)*
Tel. 01 43 54 55 27
familiahotel.com
An attractive family-run hotel with exposed beams and stonework. Some rooms on the fifth and sixth floors have a view of Notre-Dame. Next door, the more expensive Hôtel Minerve, owned by the same people, offers more spacious rooms (some can sleep five). €86–127.

Mama Shelter (I E2)
→ *109, rue de Bagnolet (20th); Tel. 01 43 48 48 48*
mamashelter.com
A state-of-the-art hotel in a former parking lot, in the up-and-coming district of St-Blaise. It has 170 rooms (each with a 24-inch wall-mounted iMac for TV, CD/DVD player, free internet access) and a fantastic avant-garde restaurant-lounge, all the work of the genius of contemporary interior design: Philippe Starck. €88–199.

Hôtel Jeanne d'Arc (B E4)
→ *3, rue de Jarente (4th)*
Tel. 01 48 87 62 11
hoteljeannedarc.com
This quiet 17th-century hotel, at the corner of a pretty street in Le Marais district, has 35 simple and clean rooms. €90–116.

Hôtel du Globe (A B2)
→ *15, rue des Quatre-Vents (6th); Tel. 01 43 26 35 50*
hotel-du-globe.fr

An elegant hotel in a 17th-century building in the heart of St-Germain-des-Prés. Stylish but slightly eccentric feudal decor: floral drapes, armors and swords, four-poster beds, stonework and exposed beams. €90–160.

Royal Fromentin (D B4)
→ *11, rue Fromentin (9th)*
Tel. 01 48 74 85 93
hotelroyalfromentin.com
Wood paneling, the wrought-iron elevator and friendly staff all contribute to the charm of this hotel. The rooms on and above the fifth floor have views of the rooftops and the Sacré-Cœur – nos 52, 54 and 66 even have a balcony. The seven-storey triple rooms overlook all of Paris. €102–179.

La Maison Montparnasse (G A4)
→ *53, rue de Gergovie (14th)*
Tel. 01 45 42 11 39
lamaisonmontparnasse.com

TRAINS, STATIONS

SNCF Information
National rail
→ *Tel. 36 35*
voyages-sncf.com
Suburban network
→ *Tel. 08 90 36 10 10*
transilien.com
Train stations
Six stations for suburban and national network: Gare du Nord (north), Gare de l'Est (northeast), Gare de Lyon (south-east), Gare d'Austerlitz (southwest, southeast), Gare Montparnasse (west, southwest), Gare St-Lazare (northwest).
TGV (Train à grande vitesse) links Paris to several major cities in France and Europe.
Thalys
Paris–Amsterdam in 3 hrs 20 mins; Paris–Brussels in 1 hr 20 mins.
Eurostar
Paris–London in 2 ¼ hrs.

TAXIS

White sign 'Taxi': the taxi is free; small orange light: the taxi is in use. Taxis are usually hard to find on Saturday nights.
Taxis G7
→ *Tel. 01 47 39 47 39*
Taxis bleus
→ *Tel. 08 91 701 010*

PARIS BY BIKE

Vélib'
→ *velib.paris.fr*
1,500 self-service rental points throughout the city. One-year membership (pay with credit card) €29; one-week €8; one-day €1.70. Rental free first 30 mins then €1 per half hour.

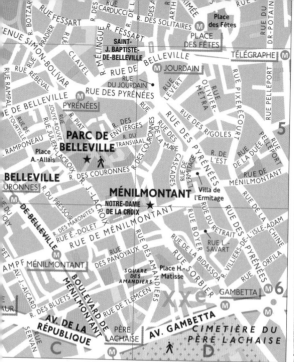

PARC DE BELLEVILLE

MÉNILMONTANT

Map I ▶

...tive process available ...eryone through ...vals, workshops, ...oitions, concerts and ...r events. Café and ...aüs charity shop.

rc des Buttes-
mont (J C4)
...es Manin and Botzaris ...; Daily 7am–10pm ...Sep; 8pm Oct-April)
...nally part of ...leon III's desire to ...Paris a healthier ...to live in, this park ...enovated in 1864, ...g over slum areas and ...; the northeast of the ...al its own large area ...enery. The engineer ...Charles Alphand

transformed the former quarries, carving them into a lake and creating a series of waterfalls and streams. The paths plunge into the undergrowth, clamber up rocks and then, suddenly, open up onto higher land.

★ Butte Bergeyre (J B4)
→ 54, av. S.-Bolívar; 2, rue G.-Lardennois; 19, rue Manin (19th)
At the top of the steep steps that struggle up the hill are some pretty houses built in the 1930s on the circular site of an ancient stadium. The area still retains its village-like atmosphere and is a lovely place for a walk among

vine-clad cottages. You get romantic views over Paris and Sacré-Cœur from the Rue Georges-Lardennois.

★ Parc de
Belleville (J C5)
→ Daily 8am (9am Sat-Sun)–sunset
There is a spectacular view of Paris from the end of Rue Piat. Below, built on the buttresses of a former gypsum quarry, is the park (1988) with over 10 acres of waterfalls, ponds, lawns and all types of vegetation.

★ Belleville (J C5)
As soon as the weather gets warm, the Boulevard de Belleville swarms with people: café terraces on

the sidewalk are packed, and from the bazaars the smell of mint tea and the wail of oriental music drift out into the busy street. Rue de Belleville, which goes to the top of the hill, is a little Chinatown, with restaurants and bazaars running the length of the Rue des Pyrénées.

★ Ménilmontant (J D5)
→ Rue de Ménilmontant (20th)
Some streets here still exude charm: Laurence-Savart for its little gardens, Des Cascades for its houses and De la Mare for its quirky bridge over the Petite Ceinture railway track.

back alleys and special bike lanes on some of the quays.

→ *Some bike stations are always full, especially at night, while others are always empty... See velib. paris.fr and 'Transportation'*

Take the métro

Although Parisians moan about the rush hour, they are proud of their subway system, not only for its efficiency but also for some of its historic stations, museums in their own right, and the lines that venture above ground to reveal striking views of the city.

→ *The stations Louvre-Rivoli (copies of paintings from the Louvre), Arts-et-Métiers (designed by François Schuiten), Varenne*

(dedicated to Rodin); and lines 2 and 6, with stretches so high that you can see through the nearby windows

Go to the beach at Paris-Plage

Parasols, white sand, deckchairs, *pétanque*, refreshment kiosks, concerts and activities of all kinds – between July 20 and August 20, the banks of the Seine on the Berge Pompidou (4th) and Bassin de la Villette (19th) turn into a fully fledged beach resort.

→ *It is very crowded on weekends; nighttime is worth considering, for the party atmosphere*

Have a picnic

The arrival of spring is the cue for many Parisians to go to a park or riverbank

for a picnic, having previously stocked up on cooked meats, cheese and a baguette and a good bottle of wine.

→ *Shop in the delis on Rues Montorgueil (B B1), Daguerre (G B4), des Martyrs (D B5), Lepic (D B4)*

Browse the second-hand bookstalls

A 2-mile stretch on both sides of the river, running from the Pont Royal to the Pont de Sully, is lined with bottle-green second-hand bookstalls, 4 ft high and 26 ft wide. They are a treasure trove of old and rare books, magazines, prints, postcards, stamps and comics, embodying a tradition that has delighted bargain hunters and passersby for four

centuries.

→ *Daily approx 11.30am–sunset; many stalls stay closed on rainy days*

Go out on the town

Paris has a thriving night life, with options to suit all tastes (indie, techno, hip hop, Latin, disco), from parties on barges in the 13th (**H**) to laid-back bars on the Canal St-Martin (**J**), from the terraces of Oberkampf (**I**) to the student dives of the Latin Quarter (**A**), from the temples of house music on the Grands Boulevards (**D**) to the expensive, ultra-cool clubs of the 8th arrondissement (**E**)...

→ *Taxis are few and far between after the subway closes (2am) on Fri and Sat nights*

BATEAU MOUCHE

CANAL ST-MARTIN

MÉTRO

BUS STOP

VELIB' DOCKING STATION

PUBLIC TRANSPORTATION

RATP Information
→ Tel. 32 46
ratp.fr

Bus
→ Daily 7am–8.30pm
(12.30am for some lines)
59 lines. Reduced service
Sun and public hols.

Noctilien
→ Daily 12.30–5.30am
Night bus; 42 lines.

Tramway
→ Daily 5.30am–12.30am
One line: T3, between
Porte d'Ivry and the
Garigliano Bridge.

Métro (subway)
→ Daily 5.30am–12.30am
(1.30/2am Fri-Sat)
Nearly 300 stations and
16 lines (numbered 1 to
14) in Paris and near
suburbs (zones 1 and 2).

RER
→ Daily 5.30am–12.30am
Five fast lines (A, B, C,
D, E) across Paris and
the Île-de-France (zones
1 to 6).

Tickets and passes
Tickets
→ €1.70 single;
€12.70 for ten
On sale in subway
stations (ticket offices
and ticket machines) and
from some tobacconists.

Mobilis
→ €6.10–14.20 depending
on the zones covered
Unlimited journeys.
Valid for one day only
within the selected zone.

Paris Visite
→ €9.75–53.40 depending
on length of pass (1, 2, 3 or
5 days) and zones covered
This pass applies to all
modes of transport and
gives reduced prices to
the monuments of Paris
and surrounding area.

---

the church of St Germain
or the garden. The latter,
also a tearoom, is a haven
of tranquility. €175–220.

Hôtel du Petit Moulin (B E2)
→ 29-31, rue du Poitou (3rd)
Tel. 01 42 74 10 10
hotelpetitmoulinparis.com
Beyond its picturesque
fin-de-siècle façade,
the reception area was
formerly the oldest bakery
in Paris, dating back to the
16th century. In contrast to
this, the 17 bedrooms were
designed by Christian
Lacroix to create an
ambience that is at once
stylish, imaginative and
yet immensely
comfortable. €190.

Hôtel de l'Abbaye (A A3)
→ 18, rue Cassette (6th)
Tel. 01 45 44 38 11
hotel-abbaye.com
A small oasis of calm and
luxury housed in a 17th-
century convent with a
flower-filled courtyard

where you can breakfast in
summer. In winter an open
fire blazes in the hearth
of the bar. Forty-six rooms
and suites, one with a
terrace overlooking the
rooftops. €205–420.

Color Design Hôtel (I C3)
→ 35, rue de Cîteaux (12th)
Tel. 01 43 07 77 28
colordesign-hotel-paris.com
As its name implies, the
accent here is on design,
each floor being
decorated in its own color,
and each of the 46 rooms
being individually styled.
€235.

Hôtel des Grands Hommes (A D4)
→ 17, pl. du Panthéon (5th)
Tel. 01 46 34 19 60
hoteldesgrandshommes.com
An elegant 18th-century
hotel in a prime location,
with 31 rooms. The de luxe
ones have views of the
Pantheon dome from their
balconies. €270; special
offers on the website.

LUXURY HOTELS

*Smart dress required if you
go to one of the following
hotels for drinks or brunch*

Ritz (C D2)
→ 15, pl. Vendôme (1st)
Tel. 01 43 16 30 30; Closed for
renovation until end 2013
The sumptuous and
legendary town house
(1898) on Place Vendôme.
High tea Saturday
afternoons. €550–770.

Hôtel de Crillon (C C2)
→ 10, pl. de la Concorde
(8th); Tel. 01 44 71 15 00
An 18th-century palace,
with marble on all floors
and Baccarat crystal
chandeliers. €770.

Four Seasons George V (B B2)
→ 31, av. George V (8th)
Tel. 01 44 71 15 00
Perhaps the most
splendid of Parisian
hotels (1928), grand
without being
intimidating. €800.

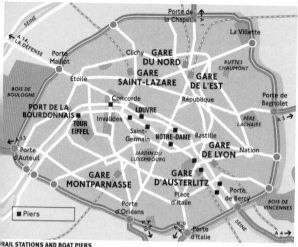
RAIL STATIONS AND BOAT PIERS

PARIS BY BOAT

Bateaux-mouches
Batobus
→ *Tel. 08 25 05 01 01*
*€15, €18, €21 (one-, two-,
five-day pass); closed Jan*
Eight stops from the
Eiffel Tower to the Jardin
des Plantes.
Bateaux-Parisiens
→ *At the foot of the Eiffel
Tower; €11*
To the île de la Cité.
Canauxrama
→ *Tel. 01 42 39 15 00*
Cruises on the canals.
**Compagnie des
Bateaux-Mouches**
→ *Tel. 01 42 25 96 10*
bateaux-mouches.fr
For lunch or dinner on
the Seine.

A small modern hotel of great charm, decorated in appealing colors: purple, magenta, yellow and orange. Excellent buffet breakfast (€9, served until noon). €109–130.
Ermitage Hôtel (D B3)
→ *24, rue Lamarck (18th)
Tel. 01 42 64 79 22
ermitagesacrecoeur.fr*
An elegant 19th-century town house with 11 stylish bedrooms – some with amazing views over Paris – beautiful printed fabrics on the walls, massive carved wooden beds and gorgeous garden. €110.
Hôtel Chopin (D C6)
→ *46, passage Jouffroy (9th) entrance 10, bd Montmartre Tel. 01 47 70 58 10 hotelchopin.fr*
A 36-room hotel dating back to 1846, hidden away at the end of a pretty shopping arcade with glass roof, close to the grands Boulevards. The

rooms (with shower or bath) overlook courtyards and roofs, and are quiet. Very friendly. €114–136.
Hôtel des Grandes Écoles (A D4)
→ *75, rue du Cardinal-Lemoine (5th)
Tel. 01 43 26 79 23
hotel-grandes-ecoles.com*
A rare thing: a villa resembling a country manor, with a private garden in the middle of Paris. The decor of this 19th-century bourgeois house is immaculate: antique furniture, floral wallpaper. You can enjoy complete peace and quiet and a large terrace for sunbathing. €115–140.

OVER €140

Hôtel Villa Mazarin (C D3)
→ *6, rue des Archives (4th)
Tel. 01 53 01 90 90
villamalraux.com*

This 1850 Haussmann building is in a splendid location, in the heart of Le Marais, and its 30 rooms are twice as spacious as they usually are in that part of town. From €140.
Hôtel des Jardins du Luxembourg (A C4)
→ *5, impasse Royer-Collard (5th); Tel. 01 40 46 08 88
les-jardins-du-luxembourg.com*
A splendid hotel in a cul-de-sac furnished throughout with exquisite taste: kilims, wood-paneling, balconies for 9 of the 26 rooms, flowers and tiling give the rooms immense charm. Separate entrance for rooms no. 1 (very spacious) and no. 27. Sauna. €143–175.
Hôtel de Londres Eiffel (F E1)
→ *1, rue Augereau (7th)
Tel. 01 45 51 63 02
londres-eiffel.com*
The French idea of an

English country cottage, with 30 small but beautifully decorated bedrooms, four of which overlook the Eiffel Tower. €145–195.
Hôtel Amour (D B5)
→ *8, rue de Navarin (9th)
Tel. 01 48 78 31 80
hotelamourparis.fr*
An unusual hotel with 24 rooms designed by artists or by the owners themselves, and decorated with all kinds of unusual paraphernalia discovered in flea markets. It has a terraced winter garden and a wildly popular café-restaurant. €150.
Hôtel des Marronniers (A B2)
→ *21, rue Jacob (6th)
Tel. 01 43 25 30 60
hotel-marronniers.com*
A hotel full of charm and character in a pretty street lined with antique shops. Rooms open onto the courtyard, the bell tower of

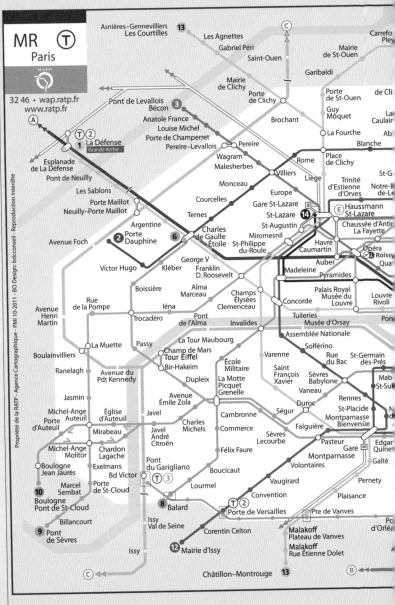

MR Ⓣ
Paris

RATP

32 46 · wap.ratp.fr
www.ratp.fr

Ⓐ

Propriété de la RATP - Agence Cartographique - PMI 10-2011 - BO Design: bdcconseil - Reproduction interdite

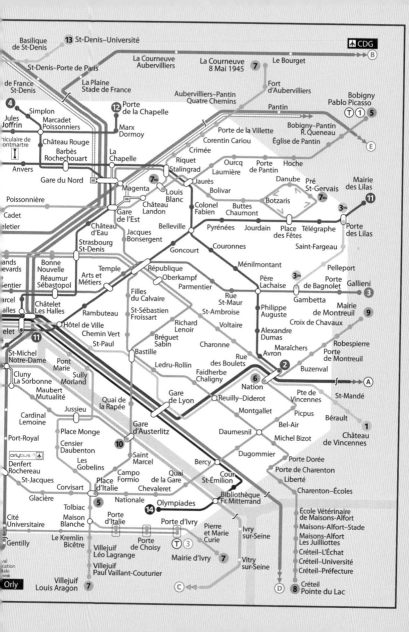

The names of streets, monuments and places to visit are listed alphabetically. They are followed by one or several map references (**F** A3), whose first letter in bold refers to the corresponding area and map.